OTHER BOOKS BY
QUENTIN COPE

Fiction
Nostradamus: The Last Christmas
The Unicorn Conspiracy
Deliver By Moonlight
The Geneveh Project
Rosalind
The Doksany Legacy

Non-Fiction
The Writers Useful Compendium
501 Writers Useful Phrases
501 *'MORE'* Writers Useful Phrases
501 Writers One-Liners
101 Fiction Writing Tips

Biography (Joint Authorship)
Tony Collins – Football Master Spy

This book is a collection of phrases, sayings, quotations and written expressions, many of which may be in common use, compiled and edited by the author of this work.

CONTENTS

:Introduction:

Useful Phrases Section

Useful One-Liner's Section

Introduction

This compendium of phrases and one-liner's is a collection of the highly successful '501 Writers' series of books including '501 Writers Useful Phrases, 501 More Writers Useful Phrases and 501 Writers One-Liner's. Owning the Compendium is much better value than buying the three books individually and as part of this particular collection, a bonus of 50 mixed phrases and one-liner's have been added. Each section shown in the 'Useful Phrases' index contains 100 entries, except for the bonus 50, and the 'One-Liner's' complete subject section contains a total of 500 entries. This is a most 'useful' volume to have on the shelf for fiction and non-fiction writers, speakers and speech writers, students at all levels, wordsmiths and journalists and all those just interested in 'words'!

Each indexed section includes a descriptive heading advising the reader about general content.

USEFUL PHRASES SECTIONS

Appearance & Looks: This section provides some phrases and descriptive lines relating to how a character ... or part of the body of a character (looks) looked or (appears) appeared. It contains references to facial expression (such as eyes, lips etc), the appearance of an individual or place and in some cases the perceived appearance of an object, real or imaginary.

Conversation: Here you will find a section of phrases and observations relating to how characters may speak, how a conversation takes place or what has been learnt or surmised from a conversation. Some phrases also refer to the perception by others of what may have been said and by whom along with some apt philosophical gems relating to the art of conversation.

Fear: This is a subject that has many parameters, but you will definitely find some phrases contained within this section to describe the kind of fear experienced by your character. As the word 'fear' means different things to different people, then so will its translation into particular expressions or perceptions, more easily described as menace or threat, many of which can be found in this section.

Feelings: This is a broad subject that attempts to describe feelings in a mix of situations. Feelings of love, belief, disbelief, passion and reflection are described to set the mood of any particular moment through the eyes of your character. Once again, you may find that certain perceptions, emotions or senses of situations and characters are directly translatable to the description of feelings and some of them are listed here.

Opinion: This is a section covering the subject of opinion, which is simply that ... Opinion! Most of the phrases in this section relate to one individual's opinion of another ... or of a particular situation. Opinion can also be classed as perception and some examples of how we perceive ourselves and others can be found here. Some phrases could be seen as philosophical and others a slightly amusing sideways look at others and varying situations.

Philosophical: There are a stack of useful quotes here covering a variety of subjects. This section is worth a regular visit as even if a particular phrase does not fit your pre-constructed scenario, there may be some that will trigger a useful line of thought. Scattering your latest work with a few philosophical gems is considered generally acceptable by editors, but the over-use of them is definitely not!

Sense: This section provides a few useful lines relating to the use of the word 'sense'. Sensing something in a scene and experiencing a sensation as a character are two different scenarios for a writer to describe or explain, so it is essential that a sensory thought is offered to the reader differently than a sensed experience. Don't forget of course that reference may be made in certain cases to that strangely evasive matter of 'common sense'!

Tenacity: This section describes situations and examples of tenacity, or lack of it, taken from a particular viewpoint, or that of others. This can be described as a certain resolve, a description of a situation of the expression of feelings. The tenacity of others can also be described in the observation of a character or the resulting change in a particular scenario. The last part of this section provides many inspirational quotations regarding the links between tenacity and success.

Time: Here are a few phrases and descriptions of 'time' as seen by a character or as viewed within a particular and relative setting. This is also about how time affects us and the scenario surrounding us as well as the waste of time and the judgment of time as it is manipulated by others. There are of course a few philosophical gems scattered here and there that will apply particularly to the single most persistent enemy of the writer … time!

Viewpoints: Everyone has a different view of a similar situation and this section provides a broad listing of views and viewpoints relating to people, situations and scenery as well as observations of one's surroundings and reflections upon one's thoughts or personal situations.

Bonus 50: This section contains a miscellaneous collection of 50 bonus phrases and the odd one-liner that have not be part of the single editions in the 501 Writer's series.

USEFUL ONE-LINER'S SECTIONS

Age: This section contains some one-liners relating to age, people's reaction to old age; the pitfalls of youth and the acceptance of middle age. It is meant to be fun and no matter how old you actually are, or feel you are, don't take it all too seriously. However, throwing one or two of these into a conversation between two characters could lift it at just the right time.

Confucius: Here you will find a section devoted to the sayings of that mythical creature 'Confucius'. If he ever did live, he would have been booked out for his entire existence at dinner parties, but of course, some of his observations on life can be quite profound. If you find yourself unable to use any of them in your writing ... you are bound to find one or two useful in your daily life.

Funny: The epitome of the one liner is the 'funny' one liner. From the 19th Century stages of music-hall to the modern day 'stand-up' comedian, the funny one liner takes pride of place. They are also an observation of real life compressing the complex realities of it into one or two simple, but sometimes profound words.

Inspirational: Any visit to a motivation seminar, anywhere in the world, can leave you feeling inadequate, with a large bill and several books filled from cover to cover with inspirational one-liners. So forget the bill and simply consult this little collection every day ... you're bound to feel better..! There are some to get you out of bed, some to help you sleep more soundly in someone else's and some to make you wish you had never thought of doing anything else but sleep in the damn thing in the first place. Be inspired ...!

Love & Emotion: This is a section covering one of the most popular of subjects and all things to do with the emotion, and all enveloping sentiment of 'Love'. However, surrounding the convictions and feelings of love are many more passions ... some we are prepared to admit to ... and others not! You'll find many of them described, sympathized with or possibly derided here ... in one form or another.

Observations: Many great men and many great women have spent a lifetime observing nature ... and necessarily ... human nature. Here are some of the results and don't forget ... "A clear conscience is usually the sign of a bad memory"

People: Well people ... this is all about YOU! ... sorry ... it's really all about US! It's about the things we do, the things we shouldn't have done and some things we got away with doing. You will definitely recognize yourself somewhere within the pages of this section ... and look out for one or two of your friends and family!

Relationships: This is the part most can identify with and some have never been able to fathom. Yes, it's that old gnawing problem of relationships and something we all have to take responsibility for. This may bring a knowing smile to more than one readers face, and for others it could be like looking in a fairground mirror.

Sex: A subject close to the heart of many ... and poorly managed by most. There are some great one-liners within these few pages ... and here is something to bear in mind: "Women might be able to fake orgasms ... but men can fake a whole relationship"

Stupidity & Fools: Everyone has a different view of a fool and many of us can remember our most embarrassing moments of complete stupidity. However, if you have conveniently forgotten, here are a few reminders.

~~~~~~

Hopefully, you the reader ... and equally importantly, you the writer, will gain something from this writer's compendium. This is not a work of academia, does not follow any particular rules of English Language teaching and each section heading should be regarded as a broad but not definitive description of its content. As already evidenced by sales of the individual editions combined here, it can make a great and popular reference, not only at the initial manuscript stage of your writing, if you are a writer at any level, but at the tough edit stage where just one small phrase adjustment can make all the difference to flow, pace, excitement and character definition.

So, to writers, readers and students of the English language and English literature everywhere …

Enjoy!

~~~~~~~~
~~~~

Part 1:
Appearance & Looks

This section provides some phrases and descriptive lines relating to how a character … or part of the body of a character (looks) looked or (appears) appeared. It contains references to facial expression (such as eyes, lips etc), the appearance of an individual or place and in some cases the perceived appearance of an object, real or imaginary.

~~~~~~

01: He had a face like a bulldog chewing a wasp

02: He/she beheld a face sunken beyond pain

03: The hard smile appeared frozen in the barrier lights

04: He/she took on a look of anticipation

05: He/she gave out a look that would quicken the pulse

06: It was a menacing look full of authority

07: It appeared, a pallor of deathly white

08: He gave out his best panty-dropping grin

09: He/she appeared as a person of porcine proportions

10: He/she was dripping, his/her clothes damp in what could only be described as a sauna-like climate

11: He/she was convinced that would put a smile on his/her dial

12: It was a smile that nearly became laughter

13: Before him, it looked like a terrifying spectre/specter

14: The appearance was that of a watery shimmer

15: He/she gazed in her/his direction with critical eyes

16: The eyes were alert and intelligent

17: The eyes appeared reduced to sharp points, ready to pierce any lies

18: They were eyes that beheld a certain shrewdness

19: The eyes told no story, staring through and beyond

20: His/her face tightened then set like a mask

21: He/she appeared far too impressed with himself/herself

22: He/she stood trapped in the sight line of glacial blue eyes

23: He/she appeared to have bookended a certain era

24: He/she looked as if he/she had received a promise from a liar

25: He/she gradually took on a generally sanguine expression

26: He/she arrived in the room; tall and moving gracefully

27: His/her eyes glazed over like a crazed windscreen

28: It was in his/her eyes, a sign of intensity

29: Is there a chin behind the beard she wondered?

30: It was a look luscious with promise

31: It was the appearance of perspiration, suddenly … like a hot shower

32: He/she appeared austere but with a haughty manner

33: He/she was either very confident, or had left the gas on

34: There was something in the eyes that made you want to look away

35: He/she appeared to be somewhere between twenty one and dead

36: He/she held a stony expression

37: He/she turned; the eyes had lost their friendliness

38: She appeared to be all over him like a rash

39: He looked to be all over her, without modesty ... like a cheap suit

40: There was the disguise of delicacy in her look

41: He/she appeared unwelcome in the room to the point of being 'persona non grata'

42: An ill disguised bitterness crept into his/her face

43: He/she possessed a charming air of vigor and vitality

44: He/she displayed a curious and inexplicable uneasiness

45: He enjoyed projecting himself as a dandified, pretty-boy-looking sort of figure

46: He/she looked a disheveled and pitifully distraught figure

47: A faint, transient, wistful smile lightened his/her brooding face

48: The darkness of the figure was captured beneath the cold glare of the chillingly desolate night

49: He/she appeared to be buried in the quick sands of ignorance

50: The eyes were shaded dull black under their precipice of brows

51: When he first appeared in her life, she knew he would become dearer to her than night to the thief

52: He/she was startled by eyes as luminous, bright and brown as waters of a woodland river

53: Then he/she was gone, disappeared - like the glow on a cloud at the close of day

54: He/she began to laugh with a sibilant sound and one that resembled the hiss of a serpent

55: He appeared to dance like a man attacked by a swarm of hornets

56: He lay still on the bed, like a warrior taking his rest

57: He saw disaster like a ghostly figure ... following her as she moved away

58: She appeared frightened - like a child in the dark

59: He/she first appeared in her/his life at a confused and troublesome time

60: His/her initial appearance was as deafening and implacable to her/him as some elemental force

61: She was viewed by many as if charm upon charm was packed into her, like rose-leaves in a costly vase

62: It appeared that to all intents and purposes, he/she was bounded by the narrow fences of life

63: His/her face appeared as imperturbable as fate itself

64: He often wondered, in regard to his appearance - if he were drop-dead handsome, and every woman he met actually dropped dead, would he ever get tired of it?

65: She knew that although all men have eyes, when focused on a beautiful woman, few have the gift of studious penetration

66: As she studied her reflection, she knew she should be grateful to the mirror for revealing her appearance only

67: He/she knew the world to be governed more by appearance than reality, feeling it as necessary to 'seem to know something' as to actually know it

68: He/she gave her/him a glance that simply flitted like a bird

69: He/she saw only a quibbling mouth that snapped at verbal errors like a lizard catching flies

70: He/she appeared to be agitated like a storm-tossed ship

71: He appeared to have an indefinable resemblance to a goat

72: An undefined sadness seemed to have fallen about her like a slowly descending cloud

73: As she spoke, a tear like silver glistened in the corner of her eye

74: His/her young eyes appeared to her/him as bright as day

75: The smile he/she softly used filled the silence like a well prepared speech

76: He looked to be as a man, who after following the plough all day, longs for supper and welcomes the sunset

77: The woman appeared with a look as austere as a Roman matron

78: They were a couple who appeared ... under close investigation, to be as close as oak and ivy

79: As she journeyed through the room, it was as if a door were suddenly left ajar into some world unseen before

80: He/she looked as innocent as a new laid egg

81: His/her expression turned as pale as any ghost

82: He looked to be at the extreme end of tension, like a well drawn bow

83: It appeared that dependency had dropped from her like a cast-off cloak

84: Emotions flashed across his/her face, like the sweep of sun-rent clouds over a quiet landscape

85: He/she suddenly became as fierce as a bear in defeat

86: His/her smile flashed with the brilliancy of a well-cut jewel

87: To her, he radiated vigor and abundance, like a happy child

88: She sat down in front of him, quaking like a jelly

89: He/she swayed in front of them, caught in the sudden grip of uncontrolled anger

90: He appeared to turn on her like a dark thunder-cloud

91: At very first sight, her beauty broke on them like some rare flower

92: Her hair was her jewel and one that hung down like summer twilight

93: Her lips had been likened to two budded roses

94: He looked upon the scene with the bland, expressionless stare of an overgrown baby

95: She fluttered her eyes, her lashes moving like fans upon her cheek

96: She spoke to him, her voice rich and vibrant, like the middle notes of a vintage 'cello

97: Indifference appeared to fall from him like a loose garment

98: The sight of her hit him like a blast from the suddenly opened door of a furnace

99: He/she appeared to her/him like a mirage, vague and dimly seen at first

100: She hovered nearby like a fluttering leaf or falling flake of snow

~~~~~~~~
~~~~

Part 2:

Conversation

Here you will find a section of phrases and observations relating to how characters may speak, how a conversation takes place or what has been learnt or surmised from a conversation. Some phrases also refer to the perception by others of what may have been said and by whom along with some apt philosophical gems relating to the art of conversation.

~~~~~~

01: It was a short conversation, followed by a Hollywood pause

02: He/she knew immediately, it was a poor choice of words

03: It was a post ironic answer

04: Although what he says is responsible, he does not want to be responsible for saying it

05: He/she spoke with an accent like warm honey

06: He/she had an attractive voice

07: He/she spoke with a cut glass accent

08: In the world of polite conversation, he/she was still developing his/her techniques

09: 'Can you more clearly define your question?' he asked archly

10: He/she could charm a tortoise out of a shell

11: He/she could talk his/her way out of a room with no doors

12: It felt like the word 'hope' had carelessly climbed out of the dictionary of conversation, packed its bags and walked away

13: It was obvious by the conversation that any level of patience had deserted him/her

14: He/she said her/his name as if holding it with tongs

15: The conversation was interrupted by the annoyingly oppressive soundtrack of everyday life

16: The words packed an unwelcome (unexpected) punch

17: He/she used words weighted with emotion

18: … and yet the explanation did not wholly satisfy him/her

19: He/she knew instantly she/he was open to persuasion

20: Did he/she presume too much in the conversation?

21: Whatever the truth, did he/she think there was anything ominous in the saying of it?

22: No matter what was being said, he/she knew that everyone would look at it differently

23: 'Forgive me if I seem disobliging in my conversation' he/she offered

24: Judging from his/her conversation, his/her sense of humor was unquenchable

25: However he/she came across, she/he would have liked to hear his/her views

26: He told her he always welcomed verbal criticism so long as it could be seen to be sincere

27: During the conversation, he/she had become curious to learn what her/his motives were

28: He/she confessed during the discussion to being a little discouraged

29: He/she confessed it was not at all in the secret of his/her ambitions

30: He/she was not capable of unraveling the intricacies of the conversation

31: During the conversation, he/she was determined not to go into any of the sordid details

32: He/she was not going to pay him/her any idle compliments

33: He/she had been persuaded by his/her candor in the conversation

34: She knew he was suppressing many of the details as he spoke

35: She was sure he could willingly pay her no higher compliment

36: She was very grateful, in fact very much flattered to hear the words

37: He was wondering if he may dare ask her a very personal question

38: He/she could not easily understand her/his undisguised astonishment

39: After listening to what had just been said, he/she could not altogether acquit himself/herself of interested motives

40: 'After such a conversation, I dare say your intuition is quite right' he/she said menacingly

41: He/she did not doubt the sincerity of her arguments, just the delivery of the words

42: He/she stated how deeply indebted he/she felt for their kindness

43: 'May I venture to ask what inference you would draw from that?' he/she asked casually

44: He/she knew from the conversation, her/his attitude would be one of disapproval

45: Now he knew by her conversation that she was being flippant

46: Of course, whatever was being said, he didn't want to press her further against her will

47: 'Please do not think I am asking out of mere curiosity!' came the quick reply

48: She/he was carefully and purposely reading between the lines of the conversation

49: She had an extraordinary gift of engaging conversation

50: He/she wanted to be persuaded by the conversation that the two cases were in fact analogous

51: He told her the older he grew, the more he listened to people who don't talk much

52: She knew that most conversations were simply monologues delivered in the presence of a witness

53: He pondered on the speed of delivery, knowing the trouble with talking too fast is you may say something you haven't thought of yet

54: He/she knew the real art of conversation is not only to say the right thing at the right time but to leave unsaid the wrong thing at the most tempting moment

55: She told him angrily that even a fish wouldn't get into trouble if it kept its mouth shut

56: He knew, before continuing the conversation, he would have to be careful of his thoughts, as they may become words at any moment

57: He sat there listening intently, knowing that silence is one of the hardest arguments to refute

58: Drawing expertly upon his/her fine command of the English language ... he/she said nothing

59: He/she was considered to be a good communicator who never missed a good chance to shut up

60: He was told discretely that the difference between a smart man and a wise man is that a smart man knows what to say, a wise man knows whether or not to say it

61: After she left the room he revealed the trouble with her was she lacked the power of conversation ... but not the power of speech

62: She advised him to keep his words soft and tender because tomorrow he may have to eat them

63: He/she stopped the conversation short on the premise when arguing with a fool ... make sure he/she isn't doing the same thing

64: She spoke in a thin shrill, piercing voice like the cry of an expiring mouse

65: She interrupted the conversation with a voice soft as sweet on the ear as a familiar tune

66: His conversation was as agile as a leopard

67: The conversation changed from one subject to another, quick as the movement of some wild animal

68: The conversation started again as sudden and unexpected as a dislocated joint slipping back into place

69: The conversation collapsed like a depressed concertina

70: He spoke eloquently; every phrase delivered like the flash of a scimitar

71: He failed to speak with the fluidity of his thought

72: The unfortunate conversation seemed to play with grave questions, as a cat plays with a mouse

73: His/her face changed with each turn of the conversation, like a wheat-field under a summer breeze

74: His/her voice cut through the conversation like a sharpened knife

75: His/her words were delivered in a near hypnotic manner, sounding like wavelets on a summer shore

76: His/her voice rose up like a stream of rich distilled perfumes

77: He/she took the scatter gun approach, his/her talk like an incessant play of fireworks

78: He stood out in the debate like a well lit moral lighthouse in the midst of a dark and troubled sea

79: He/she let words hang in the air like an eagle dallying with the wind

80: The words were as meaningless as the syllables of an unknown tongue

81: The conversation was filled with questions and answers sounding like a continuous popping of corks

82: After he spoke, she remained as quiet and as expressionless as a devout nun

83: He/she was an orator possessed of sayings that stirred the blood like the rallying sound of a military trumpet

84: He spoke in sentences level and straight like an accurately hurled lance

85: She heard him like one in a dream

86: The discussion suddenly turned to silence, a

silence that seemed heavy and dark; like a hovering storm cloud

87: Her voice came to him as soft vibrations of verbal melody

88: Sweet as music, she spoke once; then retired completely from the conversation

89: Talking and thinking at the same time came to him like the open page of a monthly magazine

90: When he joined the conversation, the strange cold sense of aloofness that had numbed her senses suddenly gave way like snow melting in the spring

91: She knew he had spoken the whole truth, naked, cold, and fatal as a patriot's blade

92: The words kept ringing in his ears, like the tolling of a distant bell

93: Unutterable words pressed on his soul like a pent-up storm craving for a natural outlet

94: She captured his attention with words like honey melting from the comb

95: Her words fell on the conversation as soft as rain

96: His words soon became a copious torrent of pleasantry

97: His mournfully delivered words provided a distorted and pessimistic view of life

98: The conversation ended up as a nimble interchange of uninteresting gossip

99: When he finally spoke, his words offered nothing more than a profusion of compliments

100: The conversation ended with a sharp difference of opinion

~~~~~~~~
~~~~

Part 3:

Fear

This is a subject that has many parameters, but you will definitely find some phrases contained within this section to describe the kind of fear experienced by your character. As the word 'fear' means different things to different people, then so will its translation into particular expressions or perceptions, more easily described as menace or threat, many of which can be found in this section.

~~~~~~

01: A cold hand closed around his/her heart

02: It had become a pulse pounding event

03: The strong smell of fear was present in the room

04: There was concern that if he/she cut of all his/her demons, his/her angels might die too

05: Death hung in the air like a suffocating blanket

06: It was fear, not visible to the eye but sharply felt in the heart

07: He knew his fear as the menace that lurks in the path of life

08: He/she was left feeling like a lost lamb in an abattoir

09: His/her heart was going like a stolen moped

10: In her fear, she knew he would give her nothing, but take from her everything

11: She was left with panic welling up inside her, a fierce blender of unwanted emotions

12: He/she stood stock still, his/her body stiff and paralyzed by fear

13: Being fearful, sometimes you have to go towards the thing that makes you want to run away

14: In his fear, sweat poured in warm rivulets down his face

15: 'Be in no doubt, I can make the sun set upon your world and you will no longer cast a shadow in it'

16: In the fear of the moment, time stands still … and yet it races

17: There was a foreboding of some destined change

18: It was a frigid touch of the hand

19: A ghastly whiteness overspread her cheek at the mention of it

20: It was a glassy stare of deprecating horror

21: His/her gaze was fixed in a grim and shuddering fascination

22: There hung in the air a haunting and horrible sense of insecurity

23: He/she felt a hint of death in the icy breath of the gale

24: A new trouble was dawning on the thickening of his/her mental horizon

25: A new, uncomfortable perplexity began to invade him/her

26: A quiver of resistance ran through him/her

27: A frightening sense of desolation and disillusionment overwhelmed him/her

28: A shiver of apprehension crisped his/her skin

29: A somber and breathless calm hung over the deepening eve

30: A stifling sensation of pain and suspense overcame him/her

31: He/she knew a thousand unutterable fears would bear irresistible despotism over his/her confused thoughts

32: There was a tragic futility in his/her actions as he/she tried to escape the fear of it.

33: He/she was left fearful and agitated with violent and contending emotions

34: In his/her fear, all the frightening unknown of the night and of the universe was pressing upon him/her

35: He/she noticed an acute note of distress in her/his voice

36: At the thought of it, he/she felt the iciness, a sinking and sickening of the heart

37: It was an immediate and obscure thrill of alarm

38: An uncomfortable premonition of fear swept over him/her

39: His/her fear went beyond the farthest edge of the darkest night

40: He/she was fearful as drowsiness coiled insidiously about him/her

41: Events were about to take an unexpected and sinister turn

42: Fear held him/her in an inescapable vice

43: In the darkness came fleeting touches of something alien and intrusive

44: In his/her fear, he/she gathered all his/her scattered impulses into one single passionate act of courage

45: It looked to be too late as a great and fearful shuddering seized upon him/her

46: He/she was haunted with a chill and unearthly foreboding

47: As he/she stood before her/him, he/she made a fearful, loathsome object

48: He/she perceived the iron hand within the velvet glove

49: Her/his heart pounded in her/his throat

50: He/she knew, in those first few seconds, he/she would have to decide if he/she wanted it more than he/she was afraid of it

51: He/she told her/him that fear is a darkroom where negatives develop

52: He/she accepted that many of his/her fears were tissue-paper-thin, and one single courageous step would carry him/her clear through them

53: His/her fear was no more than the lengthened shadow of ignorance

54: This particular fear was his/her highest fence and the question was … could he/she possibly climb it?

55: Fear made strangers of people who would normally be his friends

56: He/she felt that to conquer this fear would be the beginning of a new wisdom

57: He stated that every man, through fear, mugs his aspirations a dozen times a day

58: Fear is just your feelings asking for a hug

59: This person in front of him/her, who so feared life … was already three parts dead

60: Little did he/she know that the cave he/she feared to enter held the treasure he/she so desperately sought?

61: He/she told her/him that fear was the static that prevented him from hearing himself

62: He/she finally ran out of patience, telling her/him bluntly that he perceived fear to be the cheapest room in the house, and he/she would like to see her/him living in better conditions

63: If a man harbors any sort of fear, it percolates through all thinking, damaging his personality and making him the landlord to a ghost

64: He/she considered that fear is simply false evidence appearing to be real

65: He/she who fears to suffer, suffers from fear

66: He/she told her/him anything he'd/she'd ever done that ultimately was worthwhile... initially scared him/her to death

67: He/she knew immediately that to lead would be difficult when you're a follower of fear

68: He/she had accepted fear as a part of his/her life - specifically the fear of change. However, he/she went ahead despite the pounding in the heart that said - turn back

69: His/her fear was as fragile as a spider's web

70: He/she saw her/his fear, like a ghostly figure following her/him

71: He/she swayed back and forth in the sudden grip of fear

72: His/ her fear of her/him came and went like fireflies in the dusk

73: His/her fear, like his/her fortune melted away like snow in a quick thaw

74: The fears in his/her mind constantly murmured like a harp among the trees

75: The tingling fear kept his/her nerves thrilled like throbbing violins

76: The fear exploded on him/her like a knife-cut across the sinews of his/her not insignificant strength

77: His/her revenge overrode all his/her fears, descending perfect, sudden, like a curse from heaven

78: His/her whole fearful soul wavered and shook like a wind-swept leaf

79: Fear poured upon him/her like a trembling flood

80: It stung like a frozen lash, confirming his/her original fears

81: It was fear in confusion, like a whirling flood

82: The fear finally overtook him/her, like a caged lion shaking the bars of his/her prison

83: They ran in fear, like frightened porpoises pursued by a shoal of determined sharks

84: Conquering fear can be likened to a game in which the important part is to keep from laughing

85: He/she ran from the fearful sight, like a great express train, roaring, flashing, dashing head-long

86: His/her fear was replaced by weariness like a medieval knight worn out by conflict

87: His/her fear followed him/her like a shadow permanently cast on a fair sunlit landscape

88: His/her fear talked to him/her like a voice from some unknown regions

89: His/her personal fears were laid out before him/her like two dead lovers who finally died true to each other

90: A fear like death itself, who rides upon a thought and makes its reckless way through temple, tower, and palace

91: It was perceived as a fear much worse than dining with a ghost

92: Like great black birds, the demons of fear haunt the woods

93: The fear appeared like phantoms gathered by his/her sick imagination

94: His/her fear of failure lay heavy upon him/her like the awful shadow of some unseen power

95: He/she stood in the middle, his/her fear steadying him/her like the boar encircled by hunters and hounds

96: The initial fright had turned to abject fear, lingering in his/her life like an unloved guest

97: The fear of loneliness struck him/her like an unexpected blow

98: In his/her immediate fear, he/she remained motionless as a plumb line

99: His/her initial conception was one of fear until fear itself became a familiarity

100: He/she expected to see fear in her/his eyes but could only perceive a frightening defiance

~~~~~~~~
~~~~

Part 4:

Feelings

This is a broad subject that attempts to describe feelings in a mix of situations. Feelings of love, belief, disbelief, passion and reflection are described to set the mood of any particular moment through the eyes of your character. Once again, you may find that certain perceptions, emotions or senses of situations and characters are directly translatable to the description of feelings and some of them are listed here.

~~~~~~

01: A bewildering sense of disbelief swept over him/her

02: He/she generated a cocktail of emotions within her/him

03: He/she felt it was best described as a frustratingly 'hurry up and wait' situation

04: He/she perceived it was a light bulb moment

05: He/she could feel it was a tense and possibly near religious experience

06: It was a tidal wave of differing feelings, some of hope and some of despair, sweeping over him/her

07: He/she felt they had been left in an uncomfortable, possibly unnerving situation

08: The feeling was all thorns and no petals

09: He/she felt it was a beautiful irony

10: He/she felt that big definitely is better

11: He/she felt the bone bitingly cold

12: She had a feeling that was akin to derailing the locomotive of young love

13: He/she felt he/she was drawing comfort in his/her faith

14: He/she had a new feeling of being taken to ecstasy on a new scale

15: He/she felt the electric sensations

16: It was a new feeling; every muscle fibre/fiber, every sinew felt alive

17: He/she felt there was some wiggle room in the plan

18: It was a heart racing, heart stopping and heart breaking feeling

19: He/she felt at that specific moment that hell would be too good for such a piece of human garbage

20: He/she felt there were many unexplained holes in his/her particular tapestry

21: In this situation, he/she felt that home would be the foundation for a new beginning

22: Feeling slightly overburdened, he/she knew he/she needed to ask the question 'I can rest when I die then?'

23: He/she liked to travel light and loyalty did not fit easily into the overhead bins

24: If you are not rich, make sure you have the feeling of being rich. If you can't feel rich then you're dead

25: I'll hold a good thought for you if you feel it to be absolutely necessary

26: He felt with some measure or passion as if he needed her, like the desert needs rain

27: He/she felt that he/she was never between them, but somehow always in the middle

28: He/she would feel out of his/her depth in a puddle

29: He/she had a feeling of quivering inside

30: He/she felt relief like the passing of a gargantuan stool

31: He felt it to be no safer than shaving with a flame thrower

32: He/she could feel it slipping through his/her fingers like escaping mercury

33: It was that feeling in the pit of your stomach when you see him/her unexpectedly once again

34: He/she felt just about the drunk side of sober

35: He/she could feel the mood music of the situation was changing

36: There was a feeling, a tense feeling, heightened by the strange mournful mutter of the battlefield

37: He/she felt they would now have to throw out their heart ahead of themselves and then chase after it

38: It felt to him/her as if it was such a confused mass of impressions, like an old unused rubbish heap

39: She had a feeling he was a callous and conscienceless brute

40: He/she was feeling his/her way through a constant stream of rhythmic memories

41: There followed what felt like a great process of searching and shifting

42: He/she felt a hot up-rush of hatred and loathing toward her/him

43: He/she was consumed by a profound and eager hopefulness

44: He/she was feeling a shuffling compromise appearing, somewhere between defiance and prostration

45: He/she felt the soft suspicion of ulterior motives invading his/her thoughts

46: It was a feeling triggered unexpectedly by a tumultuous rush of sensations

47: He/she felt completely absorbed in a stream of thoughts and reminiscences

48: He/she was feeling beset by agreeable hallucinations

49: He/she felt the whole conversation to be clothed with the witchery of fiction

50: He/she felt her particular dreams and visions had been surpassed

51: She knew the most beautiful make-up for a woman was passion; but cosmetics are so much easier to buy

52: She hated him with a passion so deep, sometimes it felt much more like love

53: He had taught her to be nice; so nice that now she was completely full of niceness ... she had no sense of right and wrong, no outrage, no passion

54: He/she could not understand the science that stated 'gravitation is not responsible for people falling in love'

55: She told him, there is no surprise to a man more magical than the surprise of being loved. It is God's finger on one man's shoulder

56: The feeling of infatuation is when you think he's as sexy as Robert Redford, as smart as Henry Kissinger, as noble as Ralph Nader, as funny as Woody Allen, and as athletic as Jimmy Conners. The feeling of love is when you realize he's as sexy as Woody Allen, as smart as Jimmy Connors, as funny as Ralph Nader, as athletic as Henry Kissinger and nothing like Robert Redford ... but you'll take him anyway

57: Someone once said that love is only a dirty trick played on us to achieve continuation of the species

58: She came upon him, knowing that when love is not madness, it is not love

59: He asked one simple question. 'Do I feel in love with you because you're beautiful, or are you beautiful because I feel in love with you?'

60: He/she expressed to her/him his/her love as an act of endless forgiveness

61: To his/her way of thinking, the art of feeling love... is largely the art of persistence

62: He/she displayed a feeling of lofty remoteness

63: He/she felt distressed at the obvious ghastly mixture of defiance and conceit

64: He/she felt it was a happy and compensating experience

65: They both felt they were witnessing a hideous orgy of massacre and outrage

66: He/she revealed to her/him what he/she hoped would be seen as a keenly receptive and intensely sensitive temperament

67: His/her feelings took over the moment, breathing out an almost exaggerated humility

68: He/she felt bound up with the impossibilities and absurdities of the situation

69: He/she felt the need for a brilliant display of ingenious argument

70: He observed her, triggering feelings of a fresh and unsuspected loveliness

71: His/her suppressed feelings would finally give vent to his/her indignation

72: He/she felt he/she was falling in to the well worn grooves of intellectual habit

73: He/she felt a growing sense of bewilderment and dismay

74: He/she felt he/she should harbor his/her misgivings in silence

75: He/she had the feeling he/she was about to pour bitter and biting ridicule on his/her discomfited opponents

76: He/she was already convinced his/her plea was to be irresistible

77: He/she felt it was an impartial and exacting judgment on the situation

78: He/she felt as if he/she was being impelled by strong conviction

79: He/she left him feeling in a position of undisputed supremacy

80: He/she was left in a whirlwind of mixed feelings and saddening memories

81: He/she felt in alliance with her/his steady clearness of intellect

82: His/her feelings would have to bow in deference to a unanimous sentiment

83: What feelings are they that one experiences in moments of the most imminent peril other than those most perilous?

84: He/she felt incited by a lust for gain

85: She had more than a passing feeling he was the type of man who would be inspirited by approval and applause

86: He/she felt invested with a kind of partial authority

87: He/she felt his/her position had been laid down in a most unflinching and vigorous fashion

88: He/she felt un-attracted to lax theories and their corresponding practices

89: He/she had a feeling the whole situation was little less than scandalous

90: It was a feeling of mingled distrust and fear

91: He/she felt trapped by a mysterious and invincible darkness

92: He/she had a feeling her/his exterior was not so much polished as varnished

93: He/she felt himself/herself to be on the sure ground of fact

94: He/she was sure it was one of the foreseen and inevitable results

95: He/she felt oppressed by some vague dread

96: He/she absent mindedly felt his/her scars to remind him/her that the past was indeed real

97: The worst feeling you'll ever feel is sitting next to the person who means the world to you knowing that you mean nothing to them

98: He/she felt the success to be somewhat overshadowed by a fretful anxiety

99: She knew that despite her reserved inner feelings, she was passionately addicted to pleasure

100: He/she felt his/her patience to be under continual provocation

~~~~~~~~
~~~~

Part 5:

Opinion

This is a section covering the subject of opinion, which is simply that ... Opinion! Most of the phrases in this section relate to one individual's opinion of another ... or of a particular situation. Opinion can also be classed as perception and some examples of how we perceive ourselves and others can be found here. Some phrases could be seen as philosophical and others a slightly amusing sideways look at others and varying situations.

~~~~~~

01: It is the opinion of most women that a man wants to be a woman's first love but a woman wants to be his last

02: In his/her opinion, it was turning into a Monty Python moment

03: His/her opinion was it is better to live one year as a tiger than one hundred as a sheep

04: The opinion was it is better to travel in expectation than arrive in disappointment

05: It was purely an opinion as to the cost and benefits of a relationship

06: He/she knew he/she couldn't sell a black cat to a witch

07: Do not believe everything you have heard about me, the truth is probably much worse

08: It's only an opinion, but editing to the writer is like cleaning up after a baby, not fun but absolutely necessary

09: Everyone pretends they're something they're not to get to the place they want to be

10: He/she had a high opinion of his/her own talents

11: It was simply an opinion, but he/she could almost believe it was a good idea

12: It's a strange opinion to say she didn't know if she loved him, begging the question 'Is that something you would forget?'

13: In his/her opinion if brains were tax, he/she should be expecting a rebate

14: In his/her opinion, if there is one thing worse than being talked about, it's not being talked about

15: Impossible is merely an opinion

16: It's a rare opinion that in order to break the code, you need to start by considering everything you think you know is wrong

17: In her opinion, he had a mind like a plain brown envelope

18: In his opinion, she was nakedly ambitious

19: He/she was so crooked he/she could hide behind a spiral staircase

20: It was an opinion cloaked in ten pence psychology

21: His/her opinion was being delivered through the leaky pipe of ignorance

22: In her opinion, the only war he ever fought was the inch war

23: In her opinion, their love was like a rumor, everyone talked about it but no one really knew for sure

24: He/she felt that his/her contribution was as useful as an ashtray on a motorbike

25: What of the opinion and what thoughts are they that show the alchemy of the mind?

26: It is my opinion that you should never have a clandestine meeting in a clandestine place

27: It was an opinion contributing to a flood in the affairs of man

28: It was only an opinion, but one that appeared to contain a bewildering labyrinth of facts

29: In his/her opinion it was a disaster of the first magnitude

30: He/she offered his/her opinion with a firmness tempered by the most scrupulous courtesy

31: The opinion was simply a flourish of rhetoric

32: From the viewpoint of those who heard it, his/her opinion was a haughty self-assertion of equality

33: From his viewpoint, she displayed a keenly receptive and intensely sensitive temperament

34: His/her opinion provided a lively sense of what is dishonorable

35: In his/her opinion, it had the makings of a mercenary marriage

36: The opinion expressed was simply a nimble interchange of uninteresting gossip

37: The opinion offered was purely a patchwork of compromises

38: The opinion was delivered by a powerful and persuasive orator

39: There was a sharp difference of opinion

40: The opinion offered provided a skeptical suspension of judgment

41: He/she was opinionated and trapped in a snare of delusion

42: The verbal delivery turned out to be a somewhat complicated and abstruse calculation

43: It was only an opinion that had produced such a storm of public indignation

44: The opinion offered was a strange mixture of carelessness, generosity, and caprice

45: His/her opinion was delivered in a tone of exaggerated solicitude

46: His/her opinion seemed based on a whole catalog of disastrous blunders

47: The opinion was alien to the purpose

48: It was a brilliant display of ingenious argument

49: What was being said appeared to be calculated to create disgust

50: The opinion was one cherishing a huge fallacy

51: His/her strongly expressed opinion was that passion and prejudice governed the world, camouflaged under the name of reason

52: If she was able to hold on to this opinion, then a dead leaf might reasonably demand to return to the tree

53: In his opinion, it was an impudent trick as hackneyed as conjuring rabbits out of a hat

54: It was his/her opinion that beauty maddens the soul like wine

55: The opinion was colored like a fairy tale

56: This opinion allowed dissatisfaction to settle on his mind like a darkening shadow

57: The opinion offered was so unique it flashed with the brilliancy of a well-cut jewel

58: The voicing of his opinion left a deep and brooding resentment

59: The opinion offered proved to be an attack of peculiar virulence and malevolence

60: This biased opinion appeared to have been blown about by every peculiar wind of doctrine

61: The opinion was thankfully cleansed of prejudice and self-interest

62: He had decided that in his opinion, her statement was clothed with the witchery of fiction

63: Even under the cold gaze of curiosity it was still only an opinion

64: His opinion on the whole matter, disguised itself as chill, critical impartiality

65: His expressed opinions reflected his endlessly shifting moods

66: The opinion displayed the evanescent shades of her feelings

67: It was the opinion of many that every curve of her features seemed to express a fine but arrogant acrimony and a possibly harsh truculence

68: The opinion left them fatally and indissolubly united

69: It was only his opinion that generosity had been pushed to prudence

70: Opinionated haughtiness and arrogance were largely attributed to him

71: His initial positive opinion of her shattered as he felt the ironic rebound of her words

72: In his opinion, he found the necessary silence intolerably irksome

73: He submitted the required opinion to the others in brooding silence

74: General opinion agreed it was her stumbling ignorance which should seek the road of wisdom

75: With his opinion now fixed, it left his thoughts in clamoring confusion

76: In her opinion, he had yielded to the ingratiating mood of the day

77: The general opinion was he could have been impervious to the lessons of experience

78: His opinion was colored by the mild and mellow maturity of age

79: Opinion was somehow reflected in the indolently handsome eyes

80: The opinion he offered was due to his intense love of excitement and adventure

81: His opinion was seen to be wrong and into her eyes had come a hostile challenge

82: His various expressed opinions would lead to intimations of un-penetrated mysteries

83: The opinion had been heard and in response she sighed involuntarily

84: It was an unexpected opinion that unfortunately involved a labyrinth of perplexities

85: An opinion is a thing most infinitely subtle

86: Some opinions can eventually be proved to be a simple but bitter disillusion

87: Her well articulated opinion seemed intolerably tragic

88: In his opinion, she had kiss-provoking lips

89: His opinion would be nursed by further brooding thought

90: His well expressed opinion displayed occasional flashes of tenderness and love

91: His opinion was oddly disappointing and fickle

92: In his opinion, he was not paid to know why but to know how

93: The opinion was obviously pertinent to the thread of the discussion

94: After listening to her opinion he was left with poignant doubts and misgivings

95: The rather unusual opinion was proclaimed with a joyous defiance

96: His opinion was subject to the red tape of officialdom

97: It was just an opinion, and respect forbade downright contradiction

98: It was an opinion that was limited by the rigid adherence to conventionalities

99: In everyone's opinion, she needed to be rudely reminded of life's serious issues

100: After listening to his opinion, she assented in precisely the right terms

~~~~~~~~
~~~~

Part 6:

Philosophical

There are a stack of useful quotes here covering a variety of subjects. This section is worth a regular visit as even if a particular phrase does not fit your pre-constructed scenario, there may be some that will trigger a useful line of thought. Scattering your latest work with a few philosophical gems is considered generally acceptable by editors, but the over-use of them is definitely not!

~~~~~~

01: A man who has never lost any money, never made any money

02: A man without fear is a man without hope

03: A test of leadership is to recognize a problem before it becomes an emergency

04: Alcohol is the answer, but what is the question

05: As the purse is emptied, the heart is filled

06: Bad artists copy, great artists steal

07: Bad reviews; don't read them, measure them

08: Before a happy ever after, must come a once upon a time

09: Blood is thicker than water but a 100 dollar bill is thicker than both

10: Brevity is the soul of wit (Shakespeare)

11: Coincidences do happen, but they shouldn't happen too often

12: Courage is one virtue that without the rest is meaningless

13: Dedication creates order from chaos

14: Do one thing every day that makes you feel alive

15: Don't trouble trouble, til trouble troubles you

16: Essential writing provides essential reading

17: Every book is the possible wreck of a once good idea

18: Failure is trying but not succeeding

19: Fool me once, shame on you; fool me twice, shame on me

20: Fools never change their minds and wise men seldom do

21: Good things take time, great things happen immediately

22: Good things come to good people

23: Hating your enemy does not bring him pain

24: History has a way of delivering the right people in the right place at the right time

25: If opportunity doesn't knock, you may need to build a door

26: If things are worth doing, they are worth doing to excess (Oscar Wilde)

27: If you aim for a goal that is not your destiny, you will always be swimming against the tide

28: If you are not at the dinner, you are probably not on the menu

29: If you can imagine it, it can happen

30: If you can't give them something to love, give them something to hope for

31: If you have to project, project beyond failure

32: If you wait by the river long enough, the bodies of your enemies will float by

33: If you want to change the world, you have to live in it first

34: Imagination is more important than knowledge (Einstein)

35: Impossible dreams are simply young challenges

36: In god we trust, all others we monitor

37: In war, truth is the first casualty

38: It doesn't matter how many books you get through … It's how many books get through to you

39: It's a thin line between a blessing and a curse

40: It's not getting what you want, it's wanting what you get

41: It's not what is possible but what is probable

42: Lead, follow or get out of the way

43: Lessons not learnt in blood are soon forgotten

44: Life is about getting ahead and staying there

45: Life is about kicking ass, not licking it

46: Life is like a sewer, what you get out of it, depends upon what you put in to it

47: Love is an act of courage

48: Marriage, a good conversation that got out of hand

49: Never let the truth spoil a good story

50: Not being able to know something is no proof that it doesn't exist

51: A house divided against its self can never stand

52: A man who is his own lawyer has a fool for a client

53: A woman needs a man like a fish needs a bicycle

54: Beware of power that corrupts as absolute power corrupts absolutely

55: Age cannot wither her, nor custom stale her infinite variety

56: To those who seek it, all publicity is good publicity

57: If you ask a stupid question, you're likely to receive a stupid answer

58: One of the frustrations in life is that toast will always fall buttered side down

59: A man with one watch knows what time it is; a man with two watches is never quite sure

60: Believe those who are seeking the truth, but always doubt those who tell you they've found it

61: Every good investigator knows there's more to the truth than just the facts

62: The obscure we see eventually but the completely obvious seemingly takes significantly longer

63: Losing an illusion often makes you wiser than finding a truth

64: Sometimes it's necessary to travel a long distance in order to journey back a short distance in the right way

65: If I tell you everything that is really nothing, and nothing of what is everything, do not be fooled by what I am saying; just listen carefully and try to hear what I'm not

66: You never know 'what's enough', until you know what's more than enough

67: Men are probably nearer the central truth in their superstitions than in their science

68: Think like a man of action, act like a man of thought

69: Don't miss sight of the donut by only looking through the hole

70: To learn something new, plan to take the path you took yesterday

71: The obstacle is really the path

72: Nothing in this world really belongs to us; at best we are borrowers, at worst we are thieves

73: Remember, if you chase two rabbits, you will be likely not to catch either one

74: It is better to know some of the questions than all of the answers

75: Only in the early morning light of life can we see the world without all its shadows

76: Among creatures born into chaos, a majority will imagine an order, a minority will question the order, and the rest will be pronounced insane

77: What deep wounds ever closed without a scar?

78: Seeking the truth is not always the way to find it

79: We waste a lot of time running after people we could have caught by just standing still

80: You can't reason someone out of a position they didn't reason themselves into

81: He slept with faith and found a corpse in his arms on wakening

82: Tomorrow always comes, and today will never be yesterday

83: The weakest eyes are often fondest of the most glittering objects

84: You can see a lot simply by just looking

85: Reason and faith are both banks of the same river

86: Sometimes the questions are complicated but the answers are simple

87: He who depends on another man's table will often dine late

88: When the pain is great enough, you will let anyone be your doctor

89: One thousand people cannot undress an already naked man

90: When I die, I will not see myself die, at least for the first time

91: The human mind is inspired enough when it comes to inventing horrors; it's when it tries to invent a Heaven that it shows itself not fit for purpose

92: It's very strange when the life you never had flashes before your eyes

93: We become aware of the void only as we attempt to fill it

94: If you understand compound interest, you basically understand the universe

95: The opposite of a correct statement is a false statement. But the opposite of a profound truth may well be another profound truth

96: Sometimes an answer not yet 'blowin' in the wind' is stirring in the breeze

97: The hardest thing to hide is something that is not really there

98: Who is more foolish, the child afraid of the dark or the man afraid of the light?

99: There are some things you have to do by yourself, and yet you can't do them alone.

100: If a man will begin with certainties, he shall end in doubts, but if he will content to begin with doubts, he shall end in certainties

~~~~~~~~
~~~~

Part 7:

Sense

This section provides a few useful lines relating to the use of the word 'sense'. Sensing something in a scene and experiencing a sensation as a character are two different scenarios for a writer to describe or explain, so it is essential that a sensory thought is offered to the reader differently than a sensed experience. Don't forget of course that reference may be made in certain cases to that strangely evasive matter of 'common sense'!

~~~~~~

01: He/she had the sense he/she continued to ponder on a cauldron of thoughts

02: He/she sensed it was purely a matter of emotional intelligence

03: The trace of perfume became a pleasant sensory 'sillage'

04: She sensed it could turn into a red mist moment

05: He sensed it would end up as a stratospheric moment

06: He/she gave out a sense of insolent charm

07: He/she sensed a need to drink and swallow gratefully

08: He/she sensed a huge, heavy rush suggesting immensity

09: He/she sensed some out of the box thinking was required

10: He/she sensed it would be like a door slamming in his/her head

11: There would always be a sense that people seem strange when you're a stranger

12: He sensed he should set aside his concerns right now, but would definitely not abandon them

13: It was a long time, in a sense six months without Sundays

14: The impression was gained in a sense, that like a doorknob … everyone had had a turn

15: It was a new sense to her, the smell of the beer laden breath that was in effect the longed for smell of freedom

16: He/she sensed that somehow the words had failed, the very language itself unable to convey its proper emotion

17: She sensed there would be no doubting his membership of the 'Ersatz Toffs'

18: Sensuous thoughts crowded through his mind

19: There was a sense of viewing the matter through the restricted telescope of memory

20: He sensed she could contain the passion in her heart no more than he could control the very breath that he took

21: It seemed to project the sense of being a burlesque feint, evading an imaginary blow

22: He sensed a bitterness creeping into her face

23: It appeared to all the senses as a cunning intellect patiently diverting every circumstance to its design

24: In the heightened senses of the moment, a fawn-colored sea streaked here and there with tints of deepest orange appeared ... and then disappeared

25: There was a sense of response, a half-breathless murmur of amazement and incredulity

26: He sensed a helpless anger simmering within him

27: He sensed he was observing a manner nervously anxious to please

28: His finely tuned senses told him a new trouble was dawning on a thickening mental horizon

29: He/she sensed the person in front of him/her was a nimble-witted opponent

30: He/she sensed a pang of jealousy not unmingled with scorn

31: From the outset, he sensed the person would reveal himself to be a profound and rather irritating egotist by nature

32: He watched, all senses alert as a quick shiver ruffled the brooding stillness of the water

33: She sensed he held a secret sweeter than the sea or sky can whisper

34: It was a sensation of golden sweetness and delight

35: A new and unwelcome sense of desolation and disillusionment overwhelmed her

36: A sense of infinite peace brooded over the place

37: A sense of repression was upon her

38: A somber and breathless calm hung over the deepening eve, alerting the senses

39: She sensed a sort of eager, almost appealing amiability

40: There followed a spacious sense of the amplitude of life's possibilities

41: It was a stifling sensation of pain and suspense

42: The sensation could be described as a sweet bewilderment of tremulous apprehension

43: She drifted off in to a sensuous and swiftly unrolling panorama of dreams

44: It was a tumultuous rush of sensations

45: He sensed a twinge of embarrassment

46: She sensed a vast sweet silence creeping through the trees

47: There was a sense of being absorbed in the scent and murmur of the night

48: He sensed an acute note of distress in her voice

49: He had the sense there was possibly an assumption of hostile intent

50: She sensed an atmosphere thick with flattery and toadyism

51: He left behind a burning sense of shame and horror

52: She sensed a conscientious anxiety to do the right thing

53: They attacked his senses providing a constant source of surprise and delight

54: She sensed there would be little more than a crumb of consolation

55: She sensed that beneath his smooth exterior lay a cynical and selfish hedonist

56: He sensed an impending disaster of the first magnitude

57: It was a fastidious sense of fitness

58: It was a sense of hideous absurdity

59: He sensed he was entering a hotbed of disturbance

60: He displayed a sense of being keenly receptive and possessed of an intensely sensitive temperament

61: She quickly obtained a lively sense of what was dishonorable

62: His initial sense of negativity quickly became a lingering tinge of admiration

63: He had a sense this could turn out to be a mercenary marriage

64: She sensed there was a modicum of truth in the statement

65: She sensed his opening conversation to be a most unreasonable piece of impertinence

66: It had become a senseless passage of extraordinary daring

67: He had a sense he would be regarded simply as a pompous failure

68: It was a sense of deepening discouragement

69: He left behind him a sense of indescribable reverence

70: They sensed a sharp difference of opinion

71: He sensed a strong assumption of superiority

72: It was a sense of welcome release from besetting difficulties

73: She sensed he would always be observant and discriminating

74: Their senses were blended with the seeds of courage and devotion

75: She sensed he was enjoying this brilliant display of ingenious argument

76: She sensed a calm strength and constancy in him

77: It would be conceded purely from a genuine sense of justice

78: She sensed he was dangerously moving toward snobbery

79: He sensed she was dazzled by their novelty and brilliance

80: A sense of diffidence began to overwhelm him

81: There was a sense the argument was essentially one-sided and incomplete

82: He sensed an exact and resolute allegiance

83: She had a sense there would be frequently recurring forms of such awkwardness

84: His senses were overwhelmed by her fresh and unsuspected loveliness

85: His senses would tumble and stumble in helpless incapacity

86: He sensed a gratuitous and arbitrary meddling in the affairs of others

87: It began with a growing sense of bewilderment and dismay

88: She sensed a happy and gracious willingness

89: There was a sense amongst the onlookers his gestures and his gait were too untidy

90: She sensed his plea would turn out to be irresistible

91: He sensed from the interest being shown, he could almost allege it as a supreme example

92: He displayed an intense sensitiveness to injustice

93: He gave out a sense of having had intercourse with a more polished society in the past

94: The sense was the involuntary thrill of a more than gratified vanity

95: His sense was this could be irrelevant to the main issue

96: There was a sense in the room that this could be a capital blunder

97: There was a sense amongst them that this must be left as a matter of conjecture

98: She sensed the line of his argument would run counter to all established customs

99: He sensed it would be a fruitless and unthankful task

100: In one sense, this was little less than scandalous

~~~~~~~~
~~~~

Part 8:

Tenacity

This section describes situations and examples of tenacity, or lack of it, taken from a particular viewpoint, or that of others. This can be described as a certain resolve, a description of a situation of the expression of feelings. The tenacity of others can also be described in the observation of a character or the resulting change in a particular scenario. The last part of this section provides many inspirational quotations regarding the links between tenacity and success.

~~~~~~

01: He approached the problem with a laser-like focus

02: He appeared to have the breaking strain of a hot Mars bar

03: He knew he would have to stick with it, even if it would not stick with him

04: He held her passport in his hand; she held his manhood in hers

05: He eventually made a decision that defined him completely

06: He was so fixed on detail, he would look for flaws in the Old Testament

07: He didn't hold a grudge; in a tenacious sort of way, he was just shy of telling people he forgave them

08: He clung on to the idea like a Jack Russell with an old sock

09: He was well aware that management of change could mean a change of management, but that was someone else's problem

10: Nobody does, but somebody has to

11: It was the only dead horse he knew who responded to flogging

12: There is a line between good and evil. He held the line, he was the line.

13: 'Doing it my way will allow us to aggregate our personal gains' he advised them firmly

14: He liked to train hard, fight easy

15: You know you're brave because even though you may lose today, you will fight tomorrow

16: He knew the path to survival was to waylay destiny and bid him stand and deliver

17: He was tenaciously untouched by the ruthless spirit of improvement

18: He was accurately described as a man of imperious will

19: He was an antagonist worth her steel

20: She had become hardened into convictions and resolves

21: He drew near to a desperate resolve

22: He threw a ton's weight of resolve upon his muscles

23: His eyes shone with the pure fire of a great purpose

24: His face lit with the indistinguishable flame of decision

25: His soul was compressed into a single agony of prayer for success

26: Seriousness of purpose lurked in the depths of her eyes

27: She boldly challenged his dissent

28: She appeared to be the embodiment of dauntless resolution

29: She stood her ground with the most perfect dignity

30: The mystery obsessed him

31: His tenacity was contained within the pith and sinew of mature manhood

32: There was a strong assumption of tenacious superiority in the man

33: He held a temper and tenacity which brooked no resistance

34: He would take relentless vengeance upon arrogant self-assertion

35: The agonies of conscious failure would not stop him

36: His tenacity was in the way that madness lays

37: The blackest abyss of despair would be unable to overcome him

38: The combined dictates of reason, experience and tenacity would see him through

39: His unwavering determination was the consequence of an agitated mind

40: As he prepared himself for what was ahead, he knew the evil was irremediable

41: The fitful and tenacious swerving of passion finally did it

42: The gratification of ambition kept him extreme and focused

43: Such steadfast determination could be regarded by some as the handmaid of tyranny

44: The innermost and most obstinate recesses of the human heart controlled her now

45: Her tenacity would overcome the jostling and ugliness of life

46: The long-delayed hour of persistent retribution was gradually coming near

47: The most exacting and exciting business would be carried out determinedly

48: It was the outcome of unerring and dedicated observation

49: It was provided by the overpowering force of circumstance and necessity

50: The primitive instinct of self-preservation kicked in

51: The difference between tenacity and obstinacy is that one comes from a strong will, and the other from a strong won't

52: The tenacious road to success is dotted with many tempting parking places

53: When the world says, "Give up," tenacity whispers, "Just one more time"

54: If you pass all the pebbles in your path, one by one, you will find you have eventually crossed the mountain.

55: When you come to the end of your rope, tie a knot and hang on

56: Consider the postage stamp: its usefulness rests in its ability to stick to one thing till it gets there

57: The greatest oak was once a little nut ... who simply held its ground

58: Perseverance is the hard work you do after you get tired of doing the hard work you already did

59: He who conquers is he who endures

60: You can't go through life quitting everything. If you're going to achieve anything, you've got to stick with something

61: The race is not always to the swift, but to those who keep on running

62: It's not that he is so smart; it's just that he stays with his problems longer than the others

63: He did not consider his perseverance as a long race; he considered it to be many short races ... one after another

64: The people who get on in this world are the people who get up and look for the circumstances they want, and, if they can't find them ... they make them

65: There is no telling how many miles a man will have to run while chasing a dream

66: Tenacity is a drop of rain making a hole in the stone not by violence but simply by falling ... again and again

67: It's often the last key in the bunch that opens the lock

68: Saints are simply sinners who kept on going

69: Life is not about how fast you run or how high you climb ... but how well you bounce

70: He knew he may not be there yet, but he is closer than he was yesterday

71: She knew that God's delays are not necessarily God's denials

72: Problems are not stop signs, they are guidelines

73: Tenacity shows not only in the ability to persist but the ability to start again

74: When your dreams turn to dust, it's time to get out the vacuum

75: Most people never run far enough on their first wind to find out they have a second

76: Tenacity lies in not letting the fear of the time it will take to accomplish something stand in the way of simply doing it

77: One door opens and as I go in I am faced with a hundred closed ones

78: Let tenacity be your engine and dedication your fuel

79: Success appears to be largely a matter of hanging on after all others have let go

80: Big shots are only little shots who keep shooting

81: Tenacity should always be considered as a pretty fair substitute for bravery

82: The history of the world is full of men who rose to leadership, by sheer force of self-confidence, bravery and tenacity

83: Luck is simply tenacity of purpose

84: Patience and tenacity of purpose are worth more than twice their weight of cleverness

85: The most difficult thing is the decision to act, the rest is merely tenacity

86: Men never cling to their dreams with such tenacity as at the moment when they are losing faith in them

87: Diamonds are nothing more than chunks of coal that stuck to their jobs

88: You don`t judge a team by its record, but its heart and tenacity, two things you either have or you don`t have

89: Great works are performed not by strength but by perseverance

90: A champion is someone who gets up, even when he can't

91: His strength lies solely in the level of his tenacity

92: If you are going through hell, to get out of it you have to simply keep going

93: Ninety-nine times, the conclusion will be false. The hundredth time you will be right.

94: You should never give up on something you can't go a day without thinking about

95: Success is failure turned inside out

96: Character is defined by what you do on the third and fourth tries

97: We must have a theme, a goal, a purpose in our lives. If you don't know where you're aiming, you don't have a goal to aim at

98: If you're not failing every now and again, it's a sign you're not doing anything very innovative

99: The man who can drive himself further once the effort gets painful is the man who will win

100: There's no scarcity of opportunity to make a living doing something you love. There is only a scarcity of resolve to make it happen

~~~~~~~~~
~~~~

Part 9:

Time

Here are a few phrases and descriptions of 'time' as seen by a character or as viewed within a particular and relative setting. This is also about how time affects us and the scenario surrounding us as well as the waste of time and the judgment of time as it is manipulated by others. There are of course a few philosophical gems scattered here and there that will apply particularly to the single most persistent enemy of the writer ... time!

~~~~~~

01: It was simply a fleeting moment in time

02: He was a man, but was he a man of his time?

03: He hope the time may come again

04: In twenty years time you may call the man you call a nerd ...Boss

05: In the passing of time, it was ever thus

06: Tempus fugit (Time Fly's)

07: Time is a leash on the dog of an idea

08: It was time and had been since pussy was a cat

09: Time is described simply as infinite, constant and unstoppable

10: Time is nature's way of making sure everything doesn't happen at once

11: Time stood still, but the world kept spinning

12: Time, a dimension in which events can be ordered from the past, through the present into the future

13: A time of disillusion followed the short conversation

14: It was a confused and troublesome time

15: It had the disenchanting effect of time and experience

16: It had become the unbroken habit of a lifetime

17: He felt that time was dissolving the circle of his friends

18: They were plodding their way through times of unexampled difficulty

19: These were well-concerted and well-timed stratagems

20: The matter was suspended amid the direful calamities of the time

21: His ideas would be borne onward by slow-footed time

22: There were startling leaps over vast gulfs of time to contend with

23: The hand of time was about to sweep them into oblivion

24: The irresistible and ceaseless on-flow of time would affect the whole project

25: He didn't need telling that the leaves of time drop stealthily

26: It was a timely effusion of tearful sentiment

27: The vast and shadowy stream of time would sweep all before it

28: There was a time in his life where he might have trod the sunlit heights

29: It appeared to her that time had passed unseen

30: All the signs of the time indicated a necessity for change

31: It would happen, but in the due course of time

32: He wanted to, but his allotted time was running away

33: He was fairly sure that by this time it will be suspected

34: Coming down to modern times would be an effort for him

35: Had he time for all that might be said? he pondered

36: He seems at times to be confused and at others be quite lucid in his delivery

37: He felt inclined sometimes just to believe

38: He knew he was trespassing too long on their time

39: He hoped by this time they were all convinced

40: She rather looked forward to a time when all would be behind her

41: He regretted that the passing of time limited him

42: He would waste no time in refuting the allegation

43: It was as if you could kill time without injuring eternity

44: Time is passing, yet I'm the one who's doing all the moving

45: Men talk of killing time, while time quietly kills them

46: For disappearing acts, it's hard to beat what happens to the eight hours supposedly left after eight of sleep and eight of work

47: Time wastes our bodies and our wits, but we waste time, so we are quits

48: A good holiday is one spent among people whose notions of time are vaguer than yours

49: The flower you hold in your hands was born today and already it is as old as you

50: He who forces time is pushed back by time; he who yields to time finds time on his side

51: Time is like the wind; it lifts the light and leaves the heavy

52: There is one kind of robber at whom the law does not strike and who steals what is most precious to men ... time

53: Time is a dressmaker specializing in alterations

54: How long a minute really is, depends on which side of the bathroom door you're on

55: Time is the corrector when our judgments err

56: Time is the coin of your life. It is the only coin you have, and only you can determine how it will be spent. Be careful lest you let other people spend it for you

57: Time heals what reason cannot

58: If you want work well done, select a busy man ... the other kind has no time

59: The future is something which everyone reaches at the rate of sixty minutes an hour, whatever they do and whoever they are

60: The inertia hardest to overcome is that of perfectly good seconds.

61: Time is the wisest counselor of all

62: There are whole years for which I hope I'll never be cross-examined, for I could not give an alibi

63: Time eventually brings an end to everything except time

64: Time is the only thief against which we can obtain no justice

65: Time is gift we want most, but ... a gift we use worst

66: Time is the longest distance between two places

67: Time is but the stream I go a-fishing in

68: The present is simply a point in your life you just passed

69: It is essential to use time as a tool, not as a crutch

70: Now is the only time there is; therefore make your now wow, your minutes miracles, and your days pay

71: The time you enjoy wasting is not wasted time

72: A man who dares to waste one hour of life has not discovered the value of life

73: Whether it's the best of times or the worst of times, it's the only time we've got

74: Many of us spend half our time wishing for things we could have if we didn't spend half our time wishing

75: He had convinced her that time is like money, the less we have of it to spare the further we make it go

76: Until you value yourself, you will not value your time. Until you value your time, you will not do anything with it

77: We have only this moment, sparkling like a star in our hand … and melting like a snowflake

78: To get all there is out of living, we must employ our time wisely

79: Whatever you want to do, do it now! There are only so many tomorrows

80: In time and space, nothing is worth more than this day

81: Half our life is spent trying to find something to do with the time we have rushed through life trying to save

82: Let not the sands of time … get in your lunch

83: Time is a great teacher, but unfortunately it kills all its pupils

84: Time is an old and firmly rooted tree and we are merely the breeze rustling its leaves

85: One must often learn a difference sense of time being one that depends upon small amounts rather than big ones

86: Much may be done in those small shreds of time which every day produces and most men throw away

87: Time is an equal opportunity employer

88: The hours that flee … and as they pass, turn back and laugh at me

89: Time is merely the cradle of hope

90: Time is what we want most, but utilize worst

91: Time can be regarded as neither friend or enemy but simply a measurement

92: Time is the only thief against which there is no justice

93: The past is gone, the future is yet to come and the present slips away even as we attempt to define it

94: The inertia hardest to overcome is that of perfectly good seconds

95: Time is a brisk wind for each hour it brings something new

96: Where is the reverse gear of time?

97: You must be warned against letting the golden hours slip by, but some of them are only golden because we let them slip by

98: Time is a fire in which we continually burn

99: What minutes? Count them by sensation and not by calendars

100: Time is merely a comfortable explanation for the space within which we exist

~~~~~~~~
~~~~

Part 10:

Viewpoints

Everyone has a different view of a similar situation and this section provides a broad listing of views and viewpoints relating to people, situations and scenery as well as observations of one's surroundings and reflections upon one's thoughts or personal situations.

~~~~~~

01: He/she observed the Palladian portico heralding the entrance

02: A Regency drawing room came in to view as they continued

03: He/she thought he saw it to be a taut expression

04: It was a view he was prepared for, deep in to the backroom sinews of war

05: Others may not have thought so, but he was as well read as a magazine in a doctor's waiting room

06: He/she knew without any further movement it could end up being the closest place to hell without getting burnt

07: He/she was observed to be convalescing from open wallet surgery

08: It was seen to be distilling the essence of female humanity

09: He/she entered the room, dreading to be noticed, yet fearing to not be visible

10: Gold as it appeared to him/her could only be described as the flesh of the sun god

11: He/she appeared from a distance as the familiar stranger

12: He/she generally dismissed any valid viewpoint when he/she had his/her beer goggles on

13: He/she displayed himself/herself to the casual observer to be so white he/she could have been a blood donor who couldn't say no

14: His/her last date was so young some said she was seen arriving by skate board

15: He/she surmised that from his look he wouldn't bite unless you asked nicely

16: It was a particular viewpoint of being good from afar, but far from good

17: He/she viewed it as being merely a grain of sand on a beach called America

18: In his/her mind, he observed rocks jutting through rolling waves of sand

19: It was the sight of a sun that simply melts over the horizon

20: He/she viewed the meager traffic passing by without observing its effect

21: From his/her viewpoint, the whole situation had become vanishingly small

22: He/she closed his/her eyes and pondered upon the things you see when you haven't got a gun

23: He/she viewed the whole matter through a prism of new understanding

24: His/her view of the situation appeared to be corrected by willful blindness

25: From a period of close observation, he/she seemed to know the cost of everything and the value of nothing

26: He/she needed to question his/her taking a slightly one-sided point of view

27: His/her views are about to be altered in many respects

28: It seemed he/she was about to take an unwelcome and pessimistic view of things

29: He/she noticed it had become a campaign of unbridled ferocity

30: He/she gave out a deep authentic impression of disinterestedness

31: He/she projected a view to others as being a figure full of decision and dignity

32: He/she noticed a flame of scarlet creeping in a swift diagonal across his/her cheeks

33: He/she saw in her/his eyes a glassy expression of inattention

34: He saw it only as a portent full of possible danger

35: He/she looked up to observe a propitious sky, marbled with pearly white

36: A quick flame leapt in his/her eyes but went unnoticed

37: As he/she watched he/she observed a shimmer of golden sun shaking through the trees

38: He/she noted the sigh of large contentment

39: He/she absorbed the near perfect silence except for a soundless breeze that was little more than a whisper

40: It appeared at first to be a strange compound of contradictory elements

41: It was presented as a super-refinement of taste

42: He/she spoke to her in a tone of arduous admiration

43: An unobserved wind had strayed through the gardens

44: As he/she entered the room, all the lesser lights paled into insignificance

45: All he/she was left with was a vague jumble of chaotic impressions

46: He/she noticed the woman across the room from him had an eager and thirsty ear

47: It was seen by most as an expression of rare and inexplicable personal energy

48: His/her view changed as he/she suddenly came across an impenetrable screen of foliage

49: He/she noticed the long suffering father appealing to the urgent temper of youth

50: The passenger looked distressed as the long train swept away into the golden distance

51: He /she observed the complete scene with bookish precision and professional peculiarity

52: In his/her view, there existed a blank absence of interest or sympathy

53: To the gathering, it seemed to be a crystallized embodiment of the age

54: Viewed from any angle, this man/woman had a great and many-sided personality

55: This viewpoint, once expressed, became a great source of confusion amongst them all

56: He/she viewed her/him with an icy indifference

57: He/she saw it as a brilliant display of ingenious argument

58: He/she seemed to be chastened and refined by the experience

59: He/she left them with the view that somewhere, there was a common ground of agreement

60: He/she knew he/she would be constrained by the sober exercise of judgment

61: He/she viewed it as an afternoon of painfully constrained behavior

62: They were expressions of unrestrained grief

63: During the conversation, he/she was viewed as being far off and incredibly remote

64: From his/her point of view fate had turned and twisted a thousand ways to abandon him in this place

65: To his/her mind, he/she was feigning signs of virtuous indignation

66: He/she observed glances and smiles of tacit contempt

67: He/she was haunted by blank misgivings

68: He/she reviewed the situation and then spoke with sledgehammer directness

69: He/she could almost allege it as a supreme example

70: From his/her point of view, the stranger had somewhat overshot the mark

71: He/she saw it as an impartial and exacting judgment

72: He/she felt impelled by a view supported by strong conviction

73: It was obviously said in deference to a unanimous sentiment

74: He/she entered the room in high good humor

75: In spite of plausible arguments he/she saw it as an attempt to bury his/her opinions

76: It seemed to him/her to be an inconceivable clumsiness of organization

77: He/she seemed to possess an inordinate greed and love of wealth

78: As he/she entered the room, he/she appeared invested with a partial authority

79: It was seen by others simply as a matter of conjecture

80: It was a view that would eventually become a link in the chain of reasoning

81: Looking at the matter by and large, the conclusion was deemed as a lofty and distinguished simplicity

82: It looked as if he had/she been lulled into a sense of false satisfaction

83: He/she did not appear to be thinking straight and maddened by a jealous hate

84: What they had witnessed was seen to be the mere effects of negligence

85: Their common view was mingled with distrust and fear

86: The view was immediate and his/her worst suspicions were confirmed

87: He/she observed as she/he was moved to unaccustomed tears

88: He/she noted she/he was not averse to a little gossip

89: He/she took a view; obstacles that are difficult are not necessarily insuperable

90: He/she was obviously at variance with facts

91: He/she was looking at it from a high view standing on the sure ground of fact

92: He/she appeared to be on the edge of great irritability

93: Our views were diametrically opposed

94: He/she walked away displaying a painful and lamentable indifference

95: His/her viewpoint was genuinely parading an exception to prove a rule

96: Whatever he/she said, was peculiarly liable to misinterpretation

97: They appeared to be pelting one another with catchwords

98: He/she seemed to be working hard to predict the gloomiest of consequences

99: To all the listeners, these seemed nothing more than proud schemes for personal aggrandizement

100: There was a quickness to conceive but not the courage to execute

~~~~~~~~
~~~~

Part 11:

Bonus 50

This section contains a miscellaneous collection of 50 bonus phrases and the odd one-liner that have not be part of the single editions in the 501 Writer's series.

~~~~~~

01: Nothing is truly known and that is how we handle doubt and uncertainty

02: It was finer than a dragonfly's knitting

03: When you are not confident of anything, you will predict disaster every day.

04: Only you can turn off the dark

05: She had a face like a short changed hooker

06: A good life is one that has chapters

07: He/she said it as if the word was new to him/her ... and he/she wasn't pleased

08: Old age is no place for sissies

09: Three things that cannot be hidden: the sun, the moon and the truth

10: A writer's passage is like a moving river leading to a sea of thoughts

11: Luck favors the mind that is prepared for it

12: Diligence is the favorite mother of good luck

13: He was firmly stuck on the horns of a dilemma

14: The heart of the matter turned out to be a matter of the heart

15: He/she was standing on the diving board of self indulgence

16: He was camp as a row of tents

17: He/she and a good meal had been strangers for some time

18: Breakfast was a joke and dinner was simply a rumor

19: He/she was academic, cerebral and self contained

20: Her pastry was shorter than a midget in socks

21: He charged forward without thought, like a wounded rhino

22: It was rush hour and he could have grown a beard in the traffic

23: The conversation was 'water font' talk

24: The nurse appeared as an angel in comfortable shoes

25: There was more heat in a snowman's shoes than in this particular relationship

26: He danced like an uncle at a wedding

27: He/she knew he/she would catch more flies with honey than with vinegar

28: Its manners that show the quality of the Prince

29: It was a particular situation that suggested his best asset would be a short memory

30: He employed the broadsword approach to conversation

31: She asked 'Is that a complement I feel sticking in my back?'

32: I want to know if you can tell me anything you can't tell me?

33: He was as useful as a pair of glasses on a man with one ear

34: You look like I could use a drink!

35: It was obvious he could be broken with a feather duster

36: It looked like the same old crap, but now you choose how to flush the damn toilet

37: He had the unmistakably flat vowels of a northern upbringing

38: The man who gets along best with women is the man who can get along well without them

39: He couldn't be straight in bed

40: To the world they may be to one person, but to one person, they may be the world

41: He had fingers in everything and fingerprints on nothing

42: He was tough when dealing with the weak, but weak when dealing with the tough

43: They steal his/her time in spoonfuls

44: That's not an opinion, its science

45: It was like trying to catch a greasy eel with an oiled glove

46: He/she wrote in sumptuous sentences

47: He/she felt it was a de-normalizing situation and particularly unforgiving

48: She was destruction disguised as seduction

49: Getting to know him/her was like constantly shoveling smoke

50: He would now need to get in some strenuous relaxation

~~~~~~~~~
~~~~

ONE LINER'S

Part 12:

Age

This section contains some one-liners relating to age, people's reaction to old age; the pitfalls of youth and the acceptance of middle age. It is meant to be fun and no matter how old you actually are, or feel you are, don't take it all too seriously. However, throwing one or two of these into a conversation between two characters could lift it at just the right time.

~~~~~~

01: Old people love to give good advice; it compensates them for their inability to set a bad example

02: I'd go out with women my age, but there are no women my age

03: Middle age is a time of life when winking at a girl is closing one eye to reality

04: When we're young, we want to change the world … when we're old we want to change the young

05: You know you're getting old when you buy a sexy sheer nightgown and don't know anyone who can see through it

06: The trouble with young writers is that they are all in their sixties

07: A woman is as young as her knees

08: You know you're getting old when you stoop to tie your shoelaces and wonder what else you could do while you're down there

09: The really frightening thing about middle age is that you know you'll grow out of it

10: The best years are the forties; after fifty a man begins to deteriorate, but in the forties he is at the maximum of his villainy

11: Middle age is having a choice between two temptations and you choosing the one that'll get you home earlier

12: Old age is when you know all the answers, but nobody asks you the questions

13: Adolescence is the age between puberty and adultery

14: Age is a very high price to pay for maturity

15: A man's only as old as the woman he feels

16: I'm at an age when my back goes out more than I do

17: Learning to dislike children at an early age saves a lot of expense and aggravation later in life

18: As you get older, the pickings get slimmer, but the people don't

19: When I turned two I was really anxious, because I'd doubled my age in a year, and I thought, if this keeps up, by the time I'm six I'll be ninety

20: People who get nostalgic about childhood were obviously never children

21: Life expectancy would grow by leaps and bounds if green vegetables smelled as good as bacon

22: You still chase women, but only downhill

23: At twenty, we don't care what the world thinks of us; at thirty, we worry about what it's thinking of us; at forty, we discover it isn't thinking about us at all

24: He was either a man of about a hundred and fifty who was rather young for his years, or a man of about a hundred and ten who had been aged by trouble

25: You know you're getting old when work is a lot less fun and fun is a lot more work

26: Middle age is when your broad mind and narrow waist begin to change places

27: Old age is being ready to undertake tasks that youth shirked because they would take too long

28: As a writer, always be nice to those younger than you, because they are the ones who will be writing about you!

29: I can still enjoy sex at 74; I live at 75, so it's no distance

30: Middle age is when you begin to exchange your emotions for symptoms

31: Anyone can get old; all you have to do is live long enough

32: Memorial services are the cocktail parties of the geriatric set

33: There are only two things a child will share willingly – communicable diseases and his mother's age

34: Middle age is that period when a man begins to shed his hair, his teeth, and his illusions

35: Old age is like everything else in life; to make a success of it, you've got to start young

36: The older you get the stronger the wind gets… and it's always in your face

37: The hands on my biological clock are giving me the finger

38: When I was a kid my parents moved a lot, but I always found them

39: If something's old and you're trying to sell it, it's obsolete; if you're trying to buy it, it's a collector's item

40: Middle age is when a woman's hair starts turning from gray to black

41: You're an old-timer if you can remember when setting the world on fire was a figure of speech

42: The comfort of turning 49 is the realization that you are now too old to die young

43: Forty is the old age of youth; fifty is the youth of old age

44: Your modern teenager is not about to listen to advice from an old person, defined as a person who remembers when there was no Velcro

45: The young are always ready to give to those who are older than themselves the full benefits of their inexperience

46: Old age is like learning a new profession; and not one of your own choosing

47: He is so old… when he was in school they didn't teach history!

48: The secret of staying young is to live honestly, eat slowly, and lie about your age

49: Fun is like life insurance; the older you get, the more it costs

50: The man who is a pessimist before 48 knows too much; if he is an optimist after it, he knows too little

~~~~~~~~~
~~~~

Part 13:

Confucius

Here you will find a section devoted to the sayings of that mythical creature 'Confucius'. If he ever did live, he would have been booked out for his entire existence at dinner parties, but of course, some of his observations on life can be quite profound. If you find yourself unable to use any of them in your writing ... you are bound to find one or two useful in your daily life.

~~~~~~

51: Confucius say... man who have hand in pockets not crazy, just feeling nuts

52: Confucius say... man in bathroom with tool in hand is not necessarily a plumber

53: Confucius say... butcher who back into meat-grinder, get a little behind in his orders

54: Confucius say... creative Chinese chef without utensils can still find ways to stir soup

55: Confucius say... man who take lady on camping trip, have one intent

56: Confucius say... geometry teacher who loses parrot, will have polygon

57:Confucius say... woman who absentmindedly answer door in her 'nightie' is negligent

58: Confucius say... impotent loser is one who can't even get his hopes up

59: Confucius say... Viagra is like Disneyland... a one hour wait for a 2-minute ride

60: Confucius say... happiness is a way station between too little and too much

61: Confucius say... woman who spend much time on bedspring, may get offspring

62: Confucius say... best way to save face, is to keep the lower part of it shut

63: Confucius say... man with chip on shoulder have wood higher up

64: Confucius say... two wrongs not make right, three lefts do

65: Confucius say... one single fact can ruin a good argument

66: Confucius say... very first doctor of dermatology, had to start from scratch

67: Confucius say... man who fish in other man's well often catch crabs

68: Confucius say… even a turtle only makes progress when it sticks its neck out

69: Confucius say… egotist is a person more interested in himself, than in me

70: Confucius say… man who is impotent will have Willy-nilly

71: Confucius say… some sex is good… more is better… too much is just about right

72: Confucius say… you see the handwriting on the wall, you're in a public restroom

73: Confucius say… diplomat is a man who can convince his wife that a fur coat will make her look fat

74: Confucius say… tis better to be pissed off than pissed on

75: Confucius say… dry cleaner who is 'in hurry' for a date, will be pressed for time

76: Confucius say… don't let your affection give you an infection – put some protection on that erection

77: Confucius say… dirty hands make your nose itch

78: Confucius say… lovers in triangle not on square

79: Confucius say… man who farts in church sits in own pew

80: Confucius say… honor your personality flaws, for without them, you would have no personality at all

81: Confucius say… he who seeks revenge should remember to dig two graves

82: Confucius say… shotgun wedding is a case of wife or death

83: Confucius say… kiss on the lips is just shopping upstairs for downstairs merchandise

84: Confucius say… woman is the only hunter who uses herself for bait

85: Confucius say… some fisherman catch their fish by the tale

86: Confucius say… definition of a true genius is a nudist with a memory for faces

87: Confucius say… it is not how deep you fish, it is how you wiggle your worm

88: Confucius say… there is no future in writing history books

89: Confucius say... grandchildren are God's reward for not killing your children

90: Confucius say... show off always shown up in showdown

91: Confucius say... at the feast of ego, everyone leaves hungry

92: Confucius say... your strength lies in your continued belief that what you just ate was indeed duck

93: Confucius say... foolish man give wife grand piano, wise man give wife upright organ

94: Confucius say... man who sleep like a baby doesn't have one

95: Confucius say... is impossible to sling mud with clean hands

96: Confucius say... who mix poison ivy with four leaf clover, have rash of good luck

97: Confucius say... do not argue with spouse who is packing your parachute

98: Confucius say... difference between pink and purple, is your grip

99: Confucius say... never cut rope that can be simply untied

100: Confucius say… every teenager should get a high school education… even if they already know everything

~~~~~~~~
~~~~

Part 14:

Funny

The epitome of the one liner is the 'funny' one liner. From the 19th Century stages of music-hall to the modern day 'stand-up' comedian, the funny one liner takes pride of place. They are also an observation of real life compressing the complex realities of it into one or two simple, but sometimes profound words.

~~~~~~

101: I used to work in a shoe-recycling shop ... It was sole-destroying

102: The good thing about lending someone your time machine is that you basically get it back immediately

103: Born free, taxed to death

104: Love may be blind, but marriage is a real eye-opener

105: Judge to prostitute: So when did you realize you were raped? Prostitute, wiping away tears: When the check bounced

106: Why is the man who invests all your money called a broker?

107: Politicians and diapers have one thing in common. They should both be changed regularly, and for the same reason

108: Evening news is where they begin with 'Good evening', and then proceed to tell you why it isn't

109: I didn't fight my way to the top of the food chain to be a vegetarian

110: The shinbone is a device for finding furniture in a dark room

111: Always borrow money from a pessimist. He won't expect it back

112: I intend to live forever. So far, so good

113: My psychiatrist told me I was crazy and I said I want a second opinion. He said okay, you're ugly too

114: Worrying works! 90% of the things I worry about never happen

115: I used to be indecisive but now I'm not so sure

116: With sufficient thrust, pigs fly just fine

117: To be sure of hitting the target, shoot first and call whatever you hit the target

118: If at first you don't succeed, skydiving is not for you!

119: Does this rag smell like chloroform to you?

120: It is hard to understand how a cemetery raised its burial cost and blamed it on the cost of living

121: Impotence is nature's way of saying "No hard feelings"

122: Alcohol is a perfect solvent: It dissolves marriages, families and careers

123: Being a vegetarian is a Native American definition for "lousy hunter"

124: 100,000 sperm and you were the fastest?

125: Stress is when you wake up screaming and you realize you haven't fallen asleep yet

126: What is the most important thing to learn in chemistry? Never lick the spoon

127: No one is listening until you fart

128: What has four legs and an arm? A happy pit bull

129: If you must choose between two evils, pick the one you've never tried before

130: I have to exercise early in the morning before my brain figures out what I'm doing

131: Constipated people don't give a crap

132: If you don't care where you are, then you're not lost

133: Ham and Eggs end up being a day's work for a chicken, a lifetime commitment for a pig

134: Why do women always ask questions that have no correct answers?

135: Why do you need a driver's license to buy liquor when you can't drink and drive?

136: Insanity is defined as doing the same thing over and over again, expecting different results

137: It was love at first sight. Then I took a second look !!

138: Two antennas met on a roof, fell in love and got married. The ceremony wasn't much, but the reception was excellent

139: Never agree to plastic surgery if the doctor's office is full of portraits by Picasso

140: Laugh and the world laughs with you. Snore and you sleep alone

141: All true wisdom is found on T-shirts

142: Depression is merely anger without the enthusiasm

143: Everything is always okay in the end, if it's not okay, then it's not the end

144: Give a jackass an education and you get a smartass

145: I drink to make other people interesting

146: I'm not normally a praying man, but if you're up there, please save me, Superman!

147: If things get any worse, I'll have to ask you to stop helping me

148: If you didn't get caught, did you really do it?

149: Make it idiot proof and someone will make a better idiot

150: Never try to teach a pig to sing. It wastes your time and annoys the pig

~~~~~~~~
~~~~

Part 15:

Inspirational

Any visit to a motivation seminar, anywhere in the world, can leave you feeling inadequate, with a large bill and several books filled from cover to cover with inspirational one-liners. So forget the bill and simply consult this little collection every day ... you're bound to feel better..! There are some to get you out of bed, some to help you sleep more soundly in someone else's and some to make you wish you had never thought of doing anything else but sleep in the damn thing in the first place. Be inspired ...!

~~~~~~

151: Failure is always temporary, only giving up makes it permanent

152: Do a little more every day than you think you can

153: The best way to predict the future is to create it

154: Trust me ... never trust someone who says "trust me"

155: Violence is the refuge of the incompetent

156: A failure is only a failure when you fail to learn

157: It's far better to happily achieve than it is to feel you must achieve in order to be happy

158: Perseverance is the hard work that you do after you get tired of doing the hard work that you already did

159: Even if you're on the right track, you'll get run over if you just sit there

160: The only way of discovering the limits of the possible is to venture a little way past them into the impossible

161: Sometimes we are limited more by attitude than by opportunities

162: Take charge of your attitude. Don't let someone else choose it for you

163: People who say it cannot be done should not interrupt those who are doing it

164: Experience is the child of thought, and thought is the child of action

165: Don't take yourself too seriously, and don't be too serious about not taking yourself too seriously

166: An optimist is a person who sees a green light everywhere. The pessimist sees only the red light. But the truly wise person is color blind

167: Those who cannot change their minds cannot change anything

168: When it's time to die, let us not discover that we have never lived

169: Things turn out best for the people who make the best of the way things turn out

170: The best way to cheer yourself up is to cheer everybody else up

171: The real voyage of discovery consists not in making new landscapes but in having new eyes

172: You can discover more about a person in an hour of play than in a year of conversation

173: Always look at what you have left rather than look at what you have lost

174: Nothing will ever be attempted if all possible objections must first be overcome

175: Optimism means expecting the best, but confidence means knowing how to handle the worst

176: The optimist sees opportunity in every danger; the pessimist sees danger in every opportunity

177: Kites rise highest against the wind; not with it

178: To be a great champion you must believe you are the best. If you're not, pretend you are

179: Keep your face to the sunshine and you cannot see the shadow

180: We are what we repeatedly do. Excellence, therefore, is not an act but a habit

181: Positive thinking won't let you do anything but it will let you do everything better than negative thinking will

182: Successful people ask better questions, and as a result, they get better answers

183: An ounce of action is worth a ton of theory

184: Do not go where the path may lead, go instead where there is no path and leave a trail

185: When you know what you want and you want it badly enough, you'll find a way to get it

186: A goal is not always meant to be reached; it often serves simply as something to aim at

187: As you think, so shall you become

188: Attitudes are contagious, so make sure yours are worth catching

189: Although it's fate that presents the circumstances, how you react depends on your character

190: For every expert there is an equal and opposite expert

191: Be critical of both new ideas and accepted wisdom

192: Try not to be a person of success, but rather a person of virtue

193: Change is not merely necessary to life ... it is life

194: Holding on to anger is like grasping a hot coal with the intent of throwing it at someone else and you are always the one who gets burned

195: Our attitude toward life determines life's attitude towards us

196: Words are plentiful but deeds are more precious

197: The best way out is always through

198: Work spares us from three evils: boredom, vice, and need

199: Be not afraid of life. Believe that life is worth living and your belief will help create the fact

200: You cannot raise a man up by calling him down

~~~~~~~~
~~~~

Part 16:

Love & Emotion

This is a section covering one of the most popular of subjects and all things to do with the emotion, and all enveloping sentiment of 'Love'. However, surrounding the convictions and feelings of love are many more passions ... some we are prepared to admit to ... and others not! You'll find many of them described, sympathized with or possibly derided here ... in one form or another.

~~~~~~

201: A girl must marry for love, and keep on marrying until she finds it

202: Every man is thoroughly happy twice in his life: just after he has met his first love, and just after he has left his last one

203: Loves conquers all things... except poverty and toothache

204: If you can't help out with a little money, at least give a sympathetic groan

205: People say that money is not the key to happiness, but I always figured if you have enough money, you can have a key made

206: What pleases men most is old wine and young women

207: The one you love and the one who loves you are rarely ever the same person

208: A solved problem creates two new problems, and the best prescription for happy living is not to solve any more problems than you have to

209: Happiness is the interval between periods of unhappiness

210: Happiness is a very small desk and a very big wastebasket

211: Love will find a lay

212: A kiss that speaks volumes is seldom a first edition

213: He who laughs ... lasts

214: The penalty for laughing in a courtroom is six months in jail and if it were not for this penalty, the jury would never hear the evidence

215: Inertia accounts for two-thirds of marriages, but love accounts for the other third

216: He who laughs last probably didn't get the joke

217: They laughed when I said I was going to be a comedian; well, they're not laughing now

218: Happiness is nothing more than good health and a bad memory

219: Misery no longer loves company; nowadays it insists on it

220: A person who knows how to laugh at himself will never ceased to be amused

221: We cherish our friends not for their ability to amuse us, but for ours to amuse them

222: A sense of humor is what makes you laugh at something that would make you sore if it happened to you!

223: Love is eventually the answer ... but while you're waiting for the answer, sex raises some pretty good questions

224: Love never dies of starvation, but often of indigestion

225: A dog is the only thing on earth that loves you more than he loves himself

226: To be happy with a woman you must love her a lot and not try to understand her at all

227: A bride is possibly a woman with a fine prospect of happiness behind her

228: Life does not cease to be funny when people die any more than it ceases to be serious when people laugh

229: A woman is the only thing I am afraid of that I know will not hurt me

230: Love is the delightful interval between meeting a beautiful girl and discovering that she looks like a haddock

231: Life is like an onion; you peel off one layer at a time and sometimes you weep

232: Love is a matter of chemistry; sex is a matter of physics

233: People who say that money can't buy happiness just don't know where to shop

234: One of the indictments of civilizations is that happiness and intelligence are so rarely found in the same person

235: Before I met my husband, I'd never fallen in love, though I'd stepped in it a few times

236: Some of the greatest love affairs I've known have involved one actor – unassisted

237: I moved to New York for my health; I'm paranoid, and New York was the only place where my fears were justified

238: In the arithmetic of love, one plus one equals everything, and two minus one equals nothing

239: Happiness is a small and unworthy goal for something as big and fancy as a whole lifetime, and should be taken in small doses

240: Ways to relieve stress: Make up a language and ask people for directions

241: Cheerfulness is the art of concealing your true feelings

242: God is a comedian playing to an audience too afraid to laugh

243: Modesty in an actor is as fake as passion in a call girl

244: No woman ever falls in love with a man unless she has a better opinion of him than he deserves.

245: Bravery is being the only one who knows you're afraid

246: Love is the triumph of imagination over intelligence

247: Love is so confusing – you tell a girl she looks great and what's the first thing you do?... turn out the lights!

248: One reason I don't drink is that I want to know when I am having a good time

249: The secret of a happy marriage remains a secret

250: Money can't buy happiness; it can, however, rent it

~~~~~~~~
~~~~

Part 17:

Observations

Many great men and many great women have spent a lifetime observing nature ... and necessarily ... human nature. Here are some of the results and don't forget ... "A clear conscience is usually the sign of a bad memory"

~~~~~~

251: We live in a society where pizza gets to your house before the police

252: War does not determine who is right – only who is left

253: The early bird might get the worm, but the second mouse gets the cheese

254: A bank is a place that will lend you money, if you can prove that you don't need it

255: Why does someone believe you when you say there are four billion stars, but check when you say the paint is wet?

256: A clear conscience is usually the sign of a bad memory

257: The sole purpose of a child's middle name, is so he can tell when he's really in trouble

258: You do not need a parachute to skydive. You only need a parachute to skydive twice

259: It's not the fall that kills you; it's the sudden stop at the end

260: Never hit a man with glasses. Hit him with a baseball bat

261: When in doubt, mumble

262: A bargain is something you don't need at a price you can't resist

263: Nostalgia isn't what it used to be

264: A TV can insult your intelligence, but nothing rubs it in like a computer

265: A bus is a vehicle that runs twice as fast when you are after it as when you are in it

266: If winning isn't everything why do they keep score?

267: Why is it that most nudists are people you don't want to see naked?

268: Good health is merely the slowest possible rate at which one can die

269: Some mistakes are too much fun to only make once

270: The discipline of writing something down is the first step toward making it happen

271: Hard work never killed anyone but why take the chance?

272: Dogs have masters but cats have staff

273: The probability of someone watching you is proportional to the stupidity of your action

274: For every action, there is a corresponding over-reaction

275: The best way to lie is to tell the truth but carefully edited

276: A conscience is what hurts when all your other parts feel so good

277: Foreign Aid translates as the transfer of money from poor people in rich countries to rich people in poor countries

278: There are no winners in life…only survivors.

279: One tequila, two tequila, three tequila, floor

280: It's so simple to be wise, just think of something stupid to say and then don't say it

281: Alcoholism is the only disease that tries to convince you that you don't have it

282: A fine is a tax for doing wrong whereas a tax is a fine for doing well

283: It's not how good your work is, it's how well you explain it

284: Efficiency is a highly developed form of laziness

285: The farther away the future is, the better it looks

286: Some of us learn from the mistakes of others; the rest of us have to be the others

287: Discretion is being able to raise your eyebrow instead of your voice

288: The trouble with doing something right the first time is that nobody appreciates how difficult it was

289: As one person you cannot change the world, but you can change the world of one person

290: Those who say it can't be done are usually interrupted by others doing it

291: A smile is an inexpensive way to change your looks

292: Failure is the path of least persistence

293: A friend walks in when everyone else walks out

294: Sometimes the best way to figure out who you are is to get to that place where you don't have to be anything else

295: Better to understand little than to misunderstand a lot

296: Honesty is the best policy but insanity is the best defense

297: It takes patience to listen ... it takes skill to pretend you're listening

298: Never tell your problems to anyone ... 20% don't care and the other 80% are glad you have them

299: A goal is a dream with a deadline

300: Few women admit their age; few men act it

~~~~~~~~
~~~~

Part 18:

People

Well people … this is all about YOU! … sorry … it's really all about US! It's about the things we do, the things we shouldn't have done and some things we got away with doing. You will definitely recognize yourself somewhere within the pages of this section … and look out for one or two of your friends and family!

~~~~~~

301: There are generally two types of people … winners and losers. Winners make it happen; losers let it happen

302: Do not argue with an idiot. He will drag you down to his level and beat you with experience

303: Light travels faster than sound. This is why some people appear bright until you hear them speak

304: We never really grow up; we only learn how to act in public

305: If you think nobody cares if you're alive, try missing a couple of mortgage payments

306: Good girls are bad girls that never get caught

307: Laugh at your problems, everybody else does

308: Never get into fights with ugly people, they have nothing to lose

309: Why do Americans choose from just two people to run for president and 50 for Miss America?

310: Some people cause happiness wherever they go ... others 'whenever' they go

311: Hospitality is making your guests feel like they're at home, even if you wish they were

312: If you are supposed to learn from your mistakes, why do some people have more than one child?

313: When you go into court, you are putting your fate into the hands of people who weren't smart enough to get out of jury duty

314: Children seldom misquote you. In fact, they usually repeat word for word what you shouldn't have said

315: By the time a man realizes that his father was right … he has a son who thinks he's wrong

316: By the time you learn the rules of life, you're too old to play the game

317: Who was the first to see a cow and think "I wonder what will happen if I squeeze these dangly things and drink whatever comes out?"

318: Friends may come and go, but enemies accumulate

319: If you can stay calm while all around you is chaos, then you probably haven't completely understood the situation

320: Experience is what you get when you didn't get what you wanted

321: Why do people keep running over a string a dozen times with their vacuum cleaner, then reach down, pick it up, examine it, then put it down to give their vacuum one more chance?

322: The probability of someone watching you is proportional to the stupidity of your action

323: Do you realize that in about 40 years, we'll have thousands of old ladies running around with tattoos?

324: We are all time travelers moving at the speed of exactly 60 minutes per hour

325: To err is human; to blame it on somebody else shows management potential

326: Materialism is buying things we don't need with money we don't have to impress people that don't matter

327: It matters not whether you win or lose: what matters is whether I win or lose

328: Progress is made by lazy men looking for an easier way to do things

329: See, the problem is that God gives men a brain and a penis, and only enough blood to run one at a time

330: Why do we press harder on a remote control when we know the batteries are getting weak?

331: Why is it called Alcoholics Anonymous when the first thing you do is stand up and say, 'My name is Peter and I am an alcoholic'

332: Every day, man is making bigger and better fool-proof things, and every day, nature is making bigger and better fools.

333: The hardest thing to learn in life is which bridge to cross and which to burn

334: A celebrity is someone who works hard all his life to become known and then wears dark glasses to avoid being recognized

335: Unless you're the lead dog, the view never changes

336: A positive attitude may not solve all your problems, but it will annoy enough people to make it worth the effort

337: The trouble with being punctual is that nobody's there to appreciate it

338: Just about the time when you think you can make ends meet, somebody moves the ends

339: Wise people think all they say, fools say all they think

340: The knack of flying is learning how to throw yourself at the ground and miss

341: Ever notice that people who spend money on beer, cigarettes, and lottery tickets are always complaining about being broke and not feeling well?

342: Sometimes the road less traveled is less traveled for a reason

343: Never attribute to malice that which is adequately explained by stupidity

344: You can easily judge the character of a man by how he treats those who can do nothing for him

345: I believe in luck: how else can you explain the success of those you don't like

346: When you stop believing in Santa Claus is when you start getting clothes for Christmas!

347: I've learned that the people you care most about in life are taken from you too soon and all the less important ones just never go away

348: There are two kinds of people who don't say much: those who are quiet and those who talk a lot

349: If you can smile when things go wrong, you have someone in mind to blame

350: I saw a woman wearing a sweat shirt with "Guess" on it...so I said "Implants?"

~~~~~~~~~
~~~~

Part 19:

Relationships

This is the part most can identify with and some have never been able to fathom. Yes, it's that old gnawing problem of relationships and something we all have to take responsibility for. This may bring a knowing smile to more than one readers face, and for others it could be like looking in a fairground mirror.

~~~~~~

351: Behind every successful man is his woman, and behind the fall of a successful man is usually another woman

352: I should've known it wasn't going to work out between my ex-wife and me, because I'm a Libra and she's a bitch

353: There's a fine line between cuddling and holding someone down so they can't get away.

354: You are such a good friend that if we were on a sinking ship together and there was only one life jacket, I'd miss you heaps and think of you often

355: Two years ago I married a lovely young virgin, and if that doesn't change soon, I'm going to divorce her

356: You know your children are growing up when they stop asking you where they came from and refuse to tell you where they're going

357: The difference between in-laws and outlaws? Outlaws are wanted

358: I married 'Miss Right'… I just didn't know her first name was 'Always'

359: My mother never saw the irony in calling me a son-of-a-bitch

360: A friend is someone who will help you move, but a good friend is someone who will help you move a dead body

361: There are two kinds of friends; those who are around when you need them, and those who are around when they need you

362: Sometimes the best helping hand you can give is a good, firm push

363: I'm multi-talented: I can talk and piss you off at the same time

364: True friendship comes when the silence between two people is comfortable

365: To err is human; to blame it on someone else is more human

366: She said she was approaching forty, and I couldn't help wondering from what direction

367: Losing a husband can be hard and in my case it was almost impossible

368: Blowing out another man's flame doesn't make yours shine any brighter, but less

369: You have two choices in life whereby you can stay single and be miserable, or get married and wish you were dead

370: Don't hate me because I'm beautiful, hate me because your boyfriend thinks so

371: The difference between divorce and legal separation is that a legal separation gives a husband time to hide his money

372: I accidently ran into my ex the other day, hit reverse and accidently ran into him again

373: Love is a canvas furnished by nature and embroidered by imagination

374: Even people who are good for nothing can bring a smile on your face, when pushed down the stairs

375: Children in the back seats of cars cause accidents, but accidents in the back seats of cars cause children

376: The reason grandchildren and grandparents get along so well is because they have a common "enemy".

377: Friends are like condoms as they are supposed to protect you when things get hard

378: If it's true that we are here to help others, then what exactly are the others here for?

379: When you are arguing with an idiot, make sure the other person isn't doing the same thing

380: Sometimes I wake up grumpy and other times I let her sleep

381: I almost had a psychic girlfriend but she left me before we met

382: Be nice to your kids as they'll choose your nursing home

383: Friends come and go but enemies accumulate

384: Friendship is like money, easier made than kept

385: I didn't say it was your fault, I said I was blaming you

386: I'm trying to see things from your point of view, but I can't get my head that far up your ass

387: If a man tells a woman she's beautiful she'll overlook most of his other lies

388: If you lend someone money and never see that person again, it was probably worth it

389: Marriage is grand, but a divorce is a hundred grand

390: Marriage is an expensive way of getting your laundry done for free

391: When a man steals your wife, there is no better revenge than to let him keep her

392: Family reunions are a time when you come face to face with your family tree, and realize some branches need to be cut

393: The last thing I want to do is hurt you … but it's still on the list

394: My parents only had one argument in forty-five years and it lasted forty-three years

395: The most important thing in a relationship between a man and a woman is that one of them must be good at taking orders

396: Dates are basically where you go out and act like someone you're not until the person likes you enough to be who you actually are

397: If you can't live without me, why aren't you dead already?

398: I went out with a guy who once told me I didn't need to drink to make myself more fun to be around, and I told him, I'm drinking so that you're more fun to be around

399: The guy I fell in love with had an easy going spirit with a fast car; but he wouldn't marry me, so I ended up with you

400: When a man's best friend is his dog, that dog has a problem

~~~~~~~~~
~~~~

Part 20:

Sex

A subject close to the heart of many ... and poorly managed by most. There are some great one liner's within these next few pages ... and here is something to bear in mind: "Women might be able to fake orgasms ... but men can fake a whole relationship"

~~~~~~

401: Sex is not the answer, sex is the question and "Yes" is the answer.

402: Having sex is like playing bridge; if you don't have a good partner, you'd better have a good hand.

403: If sex is a pain in the ass, then you're doing it wrong

404: Virginity is like a soap bubble, one prick and it is gone

405: The big difference between sex for money and sex for free is that sex for money usually costs a lot less.

406: Children in the dark make accidents, but accidents in the dark make children

407: Does time fly when you're having sex or was it really just one minute?

408: Panties are not the best thing on earth, but right next to it.

409: Remember, if you smoke after sex you're doing it too fast

410: Without nipples, breasts would be pointless

411: Men have two emotions: Hungry and Horny. If you see him without an erection, make him a sandwich

412: Women might be able to fake orgasms, but men can fake a whole relationship

413: During sex, my girlfriend always wants to talk to me, and just the other night she called me from a hotel.

414: Silence doesn't mean you're sexual performance left her speechless

415: Why is a bra singular and panties plural?

416: The last time I was inside a woman was when I went to the Statue of Liberty

417: Sex on T.V. can't hurt unless you fall off

418: You have to accept it; your parents HAVE had sex before

419: I love oral sex; it's the phone bill I hate

420: Sex at age 90 is like trying to shoot pool with a rope

421: The sex was so good that even the neighbors had a cigarette

422: A pram ... its last year's fun on wheels

423: Genitalia is NOT an Italian airline

424: A man on a date wonders if he'll get lucky but the woman already knows

425: Except for 75% of the women, everyone in the whole world wants to have sex

426: Most women don't know where to look when they're eating a banana

427: Sex is like air; it's not important unless you aren't getting any

428: Software is just like sex, one mistake and you end up giving lifetime support

429: The difference between pornography and erotica is only lighting

430: The web isn't better than sex, but sliced bread is in serious trouble

431: I told her the thing I loved most about her was her mind, because that's what told her to get into bed with me naked.

432: I'm not a good lover, but at least I'm fast

433: The kiss is a wordless articulation of desire whose object lies in the future, and somewhat to the south

434: My wife wants sex in the back of the car and she wants me to drive

435: My girlfriend always laughs during sex, no matter what she's reading

436: Women will never be equal to men until they can walk down the street with a bald head and a beer gut, and still think they are sexy

437: The trouble with incest is that it gets you involved with relatives

438: I remember the first time I had sex, I kept the receipt

439: How can we possibly use sex to get what we want?... sex *is* what we want!

440: Sex between a man and a woman can be absolutely wonderful, provided you get between the right man and the right woman

441: Marriage is the price men pay for sex and sex is the price women pay for marriage

442: Physics is like sex; sure, it may give some practical results, but that's not why we do it

443: 'Easy' is used to describe a woman who has the sexual morals of a man

444: Once upon a time, air was clean and sex was dirty

445: Some people are better imagined in one's bed than found there in the morning

446: Men love to be thought of as funny, except when they're in bed

447: The only thing wrong with being an atheist is that there's nobody to talk to during an orgasm

448: I don't think I'm good in bed; my husband never said anything, but after we made love he'd take a piece of chalk and outline my body

449: Anyone who eats three meals a day should understand why cookbooks outsell sex books three to one

450: I had group sex once, when my wife screwed me in front of the jury

~~~~~~~~
~~~~

Part 21:

Stupidity & Fools

Everyone has a different view of a fool and many of us can remember our most embarrassing moments of complete stupidity. However, if you have conveniently forgotten, here are a few reminders.

~~~~~~

451: We are all born ignorant, but one must work hard to remain stupid

452: What he lacks in intelligence, he makes up for in stupidity

453: He is so stupid… he took a blood test and failed

454: He is so stupid… when you said it was chilly outside he went and got a bowl

455: When stupidity is a sufficient explanation, there is no need to have recourse to any other

456: Some folks are wise and some otherwise

457: It is dangerous to be sincere unless you are also stupid

458: Intelligent people, when assembled into an organization, will tend toward collective stupidity

459: If there are no stupid questions, then what kind of questions do stupid people ask?

460: Only two things are infinite, the universe and human stupidity, and I'm not sure about the former

461: In view of the fact that God limited the intelligence of man, it seems unfair that he did not also limit his stupidity

462: Stupid men are often capable of things the clever would not dare to contemplate

463: In politics, stupidity is not a handicap

464: Stupidity has a knack of getting its way

465: I am patient with stupidity but not with those who are proud of it

466: Think of how stupid the average person is, and realize half of them are stupider than that

467: There are four things that hold back human progress – ignorance, stupidity, committees and accountants

468: I don't want to elect anyone stupid enough to want the job

469: Stupidity, if left untreated, is self-correcting

470: Ordinarily he was insane, but he had lucid moments when he was merely stupid

471: Never attribute to malice that which is adequately explained by stupidity

472: He's so stupid… if you give him a penny for his thoughts, you'll get change back

473: You cannot compile a wit out of two half-wits

474: Stupidity got us into this mess, and stupidity will doubtless get us out

475: One half of being smart is knowing what you are dumb about

476: Evil and stupidity are randomly distributed

477: There's nothing more dangerous than a resourceful idiot

478: The difference between stupidity and genius is that genius has its limits

479: It is said that if you line up all the cars in the world end to end, someone would be stupid enough to try and pass them

480: The word 'user' is the word used by the computer professional when they mean idiot

481: Talk sense to a fool and he calls you foolish

482: A full tongue and an empty brain are seldom parted

483: There are a good many fools who call me a friend, and also a good many friends who call me a fool

484: A word to the wise ain't necessary, it is the stupid ones who need all the advice

485: Build a system that even a fool can use, and only a fool will want to use it

486: A fool and his money are soon elected

487: People think it must be fun to be a super genius, but they don't realize how hard it is to put up with all the idiots in the world

488: Never let a fool kiss you, or a kiss fool you

489: People with narrow minds usually have broad tongues

490: A fellow who is always declaring he's no fool, usually has his suspicions

491: The trouble with the world is that the stupid are cocksure and the intelligent full of doubt

492: A pipe gives a wise man time to think and a fool something to stick in his mouth

493: Most people don't act stupid: it's the real thing!

494: One has fear in front of a goat, in back of a mule, and on every side of a fool

495: Little things affect little minds

496: A man may be stupid and not know it, but not if he is married

497: The first man to compare the cheeks of a young woman to a rose was obviously a poet; the first to repeat it was possibly an idiot

498: Wise men talk because they have something to say; fools, because they have to say something

499: Only a man who has loved a woman of genius can appreciate what happiness there is in loving a fool

500: Every man is a fool for at least five minutes every day; wisdom consists of not exceeding the limit

~~~~~~~~
~~~~

THE END